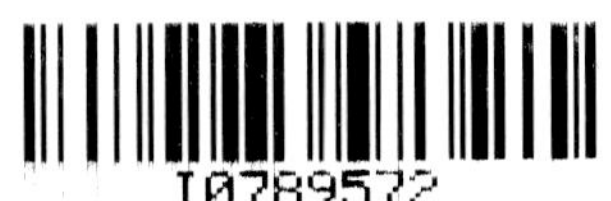

This Book Belongs to

____

Color Test Page

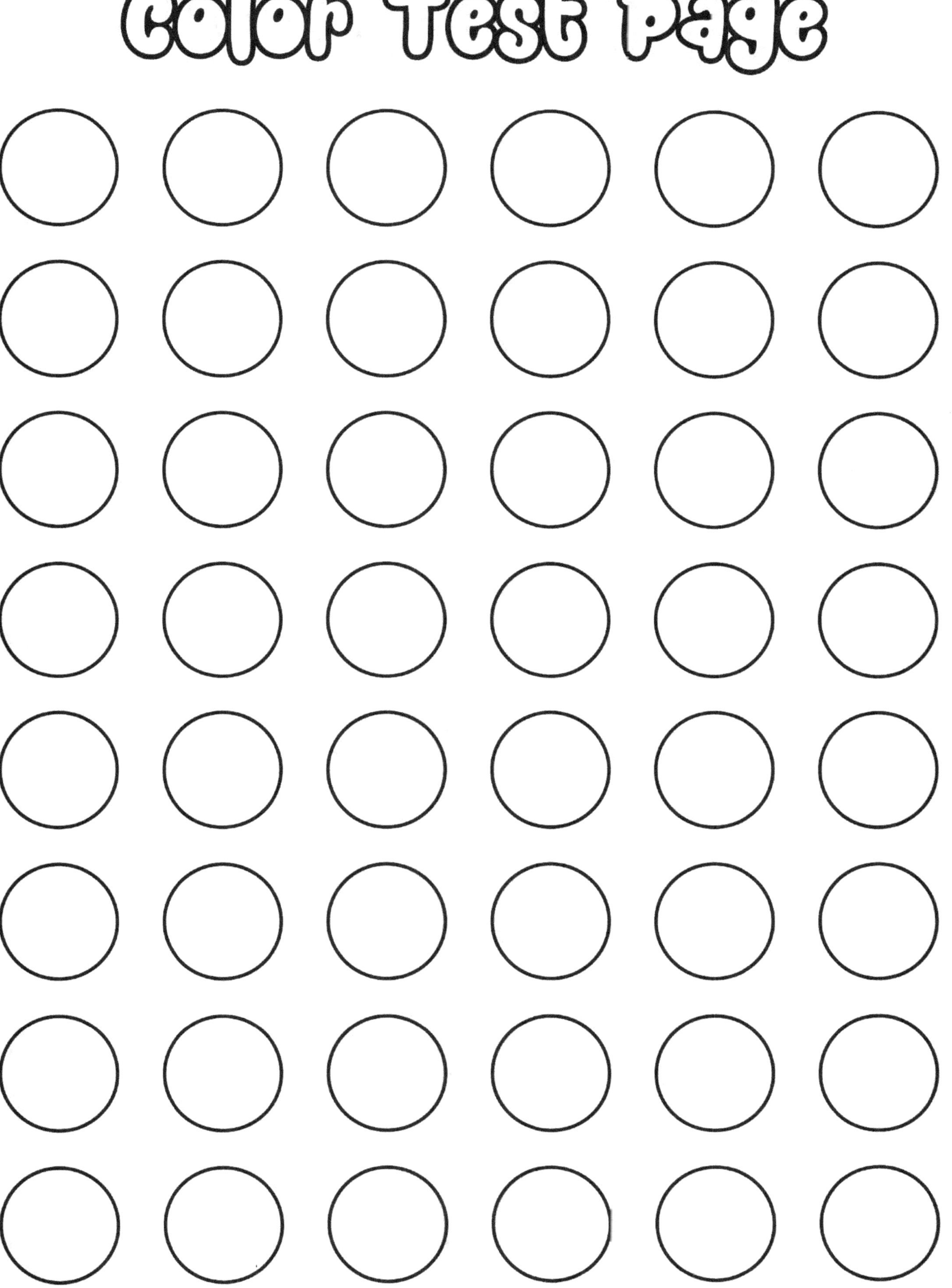

Color Test Page

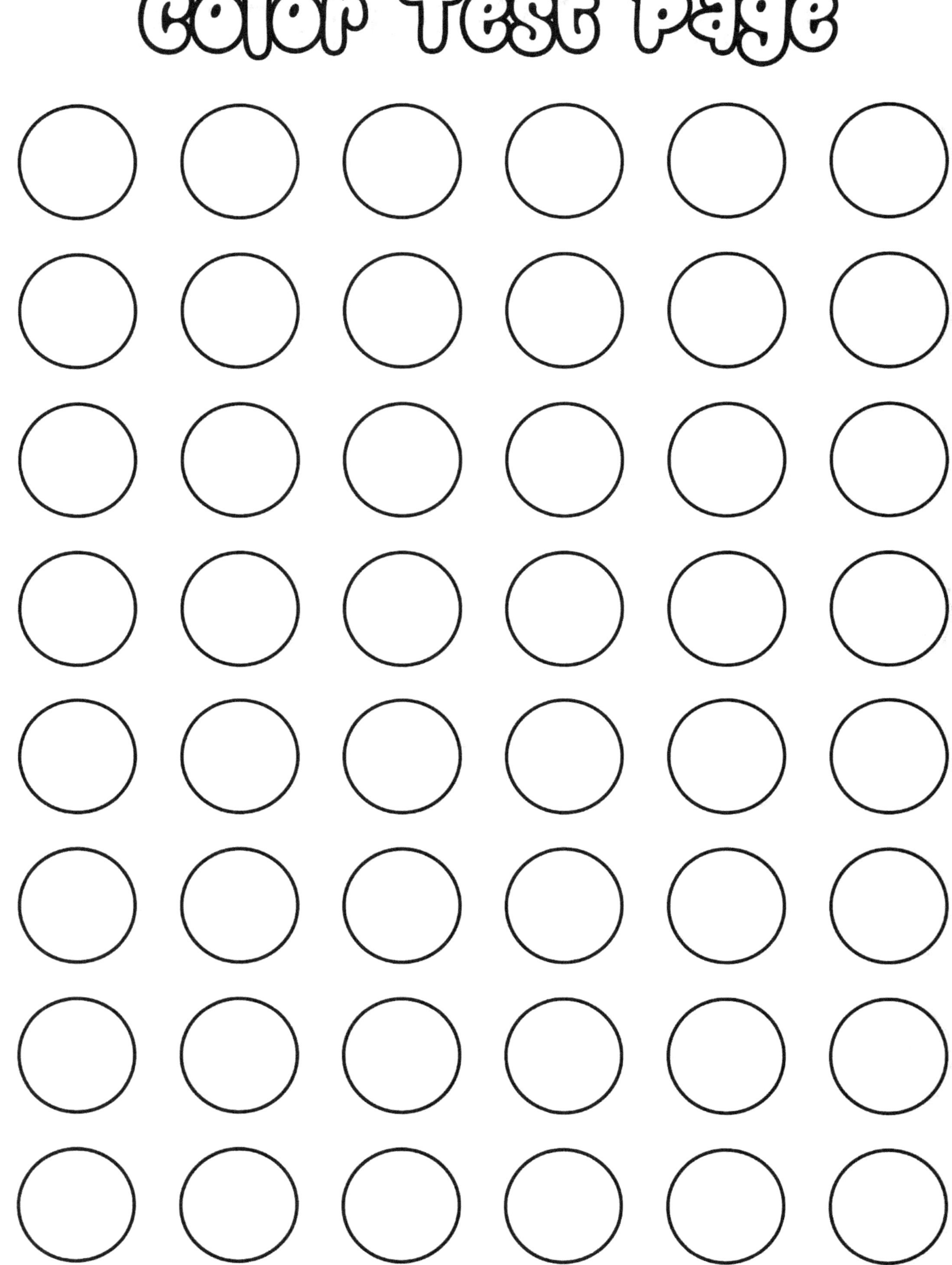

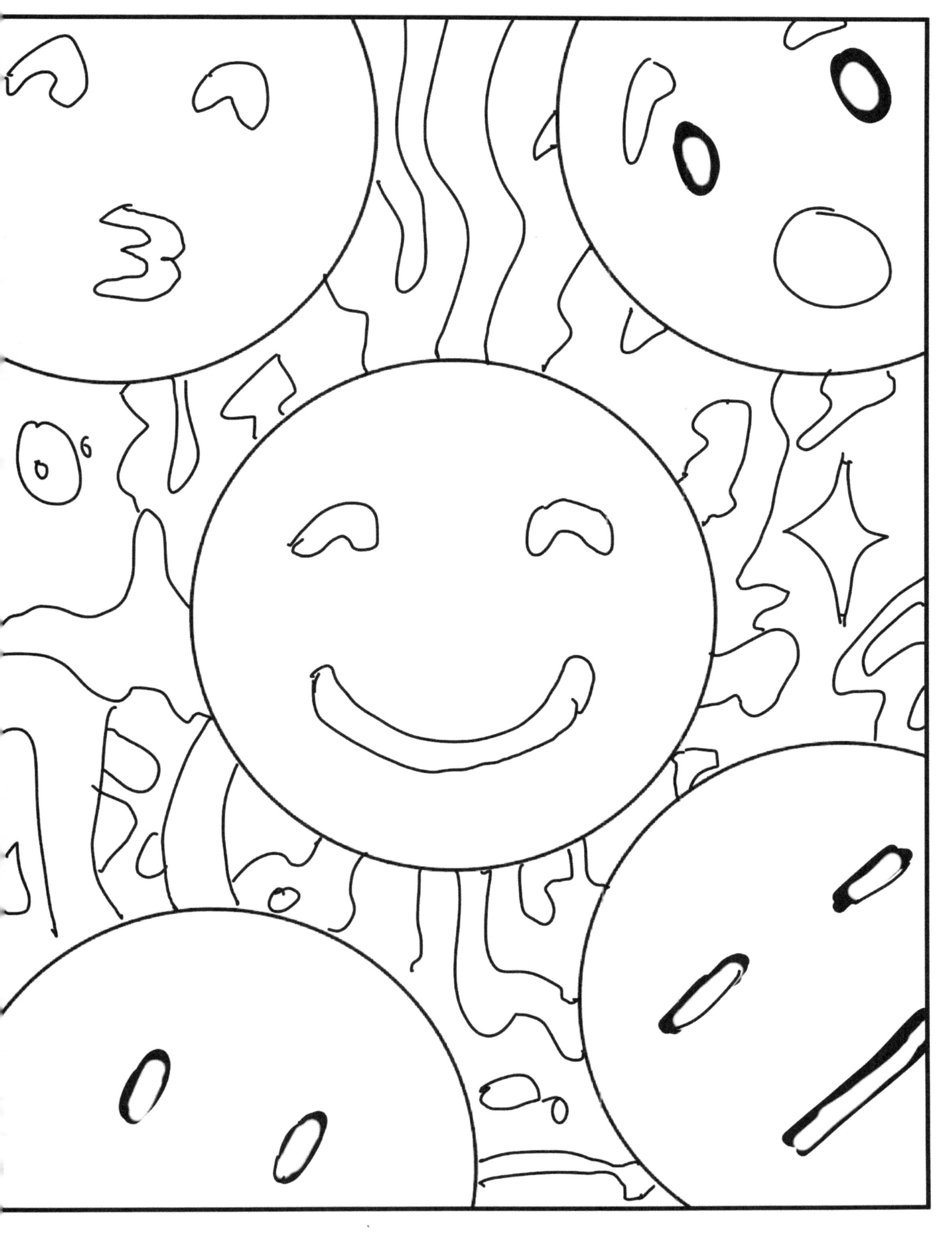

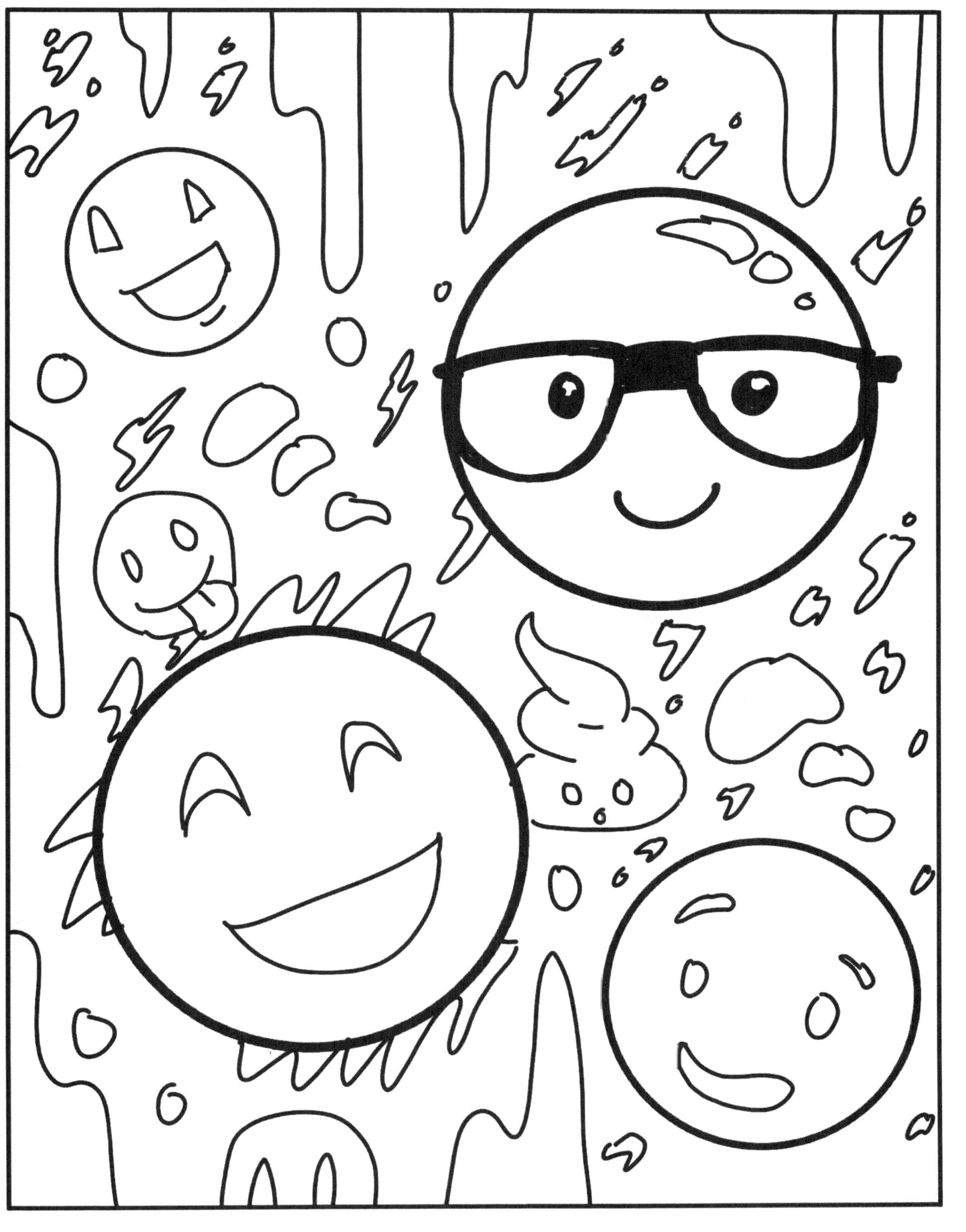

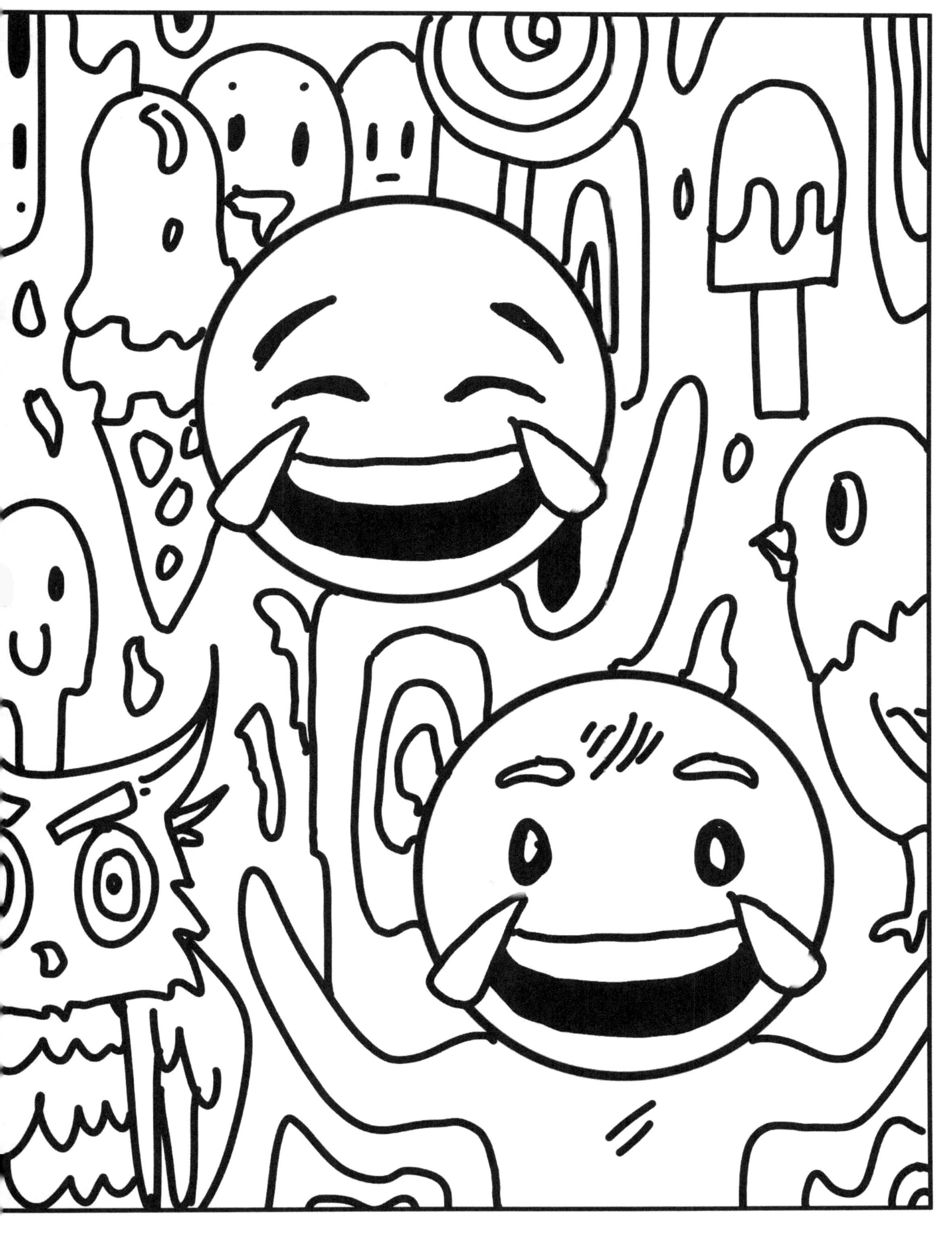

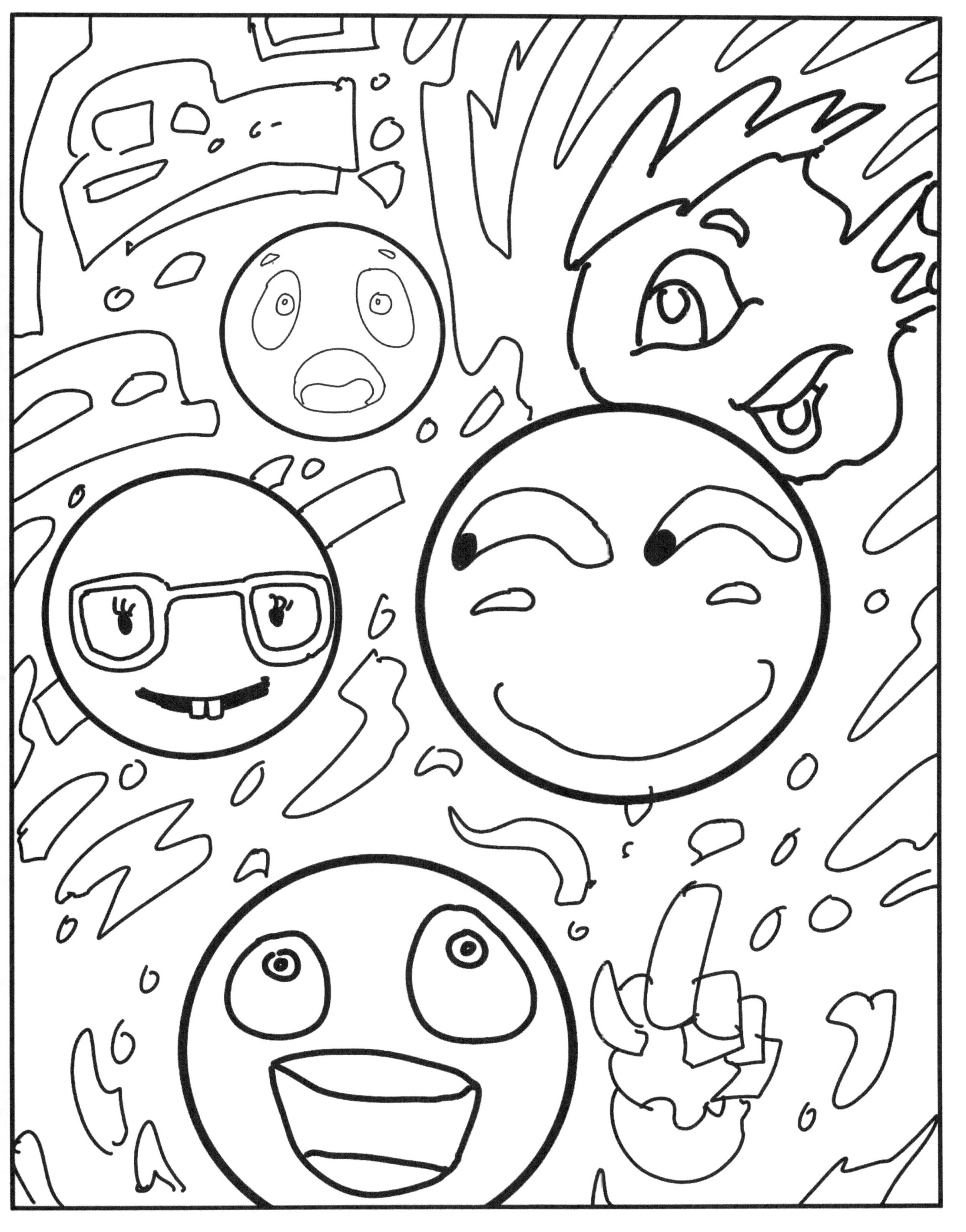

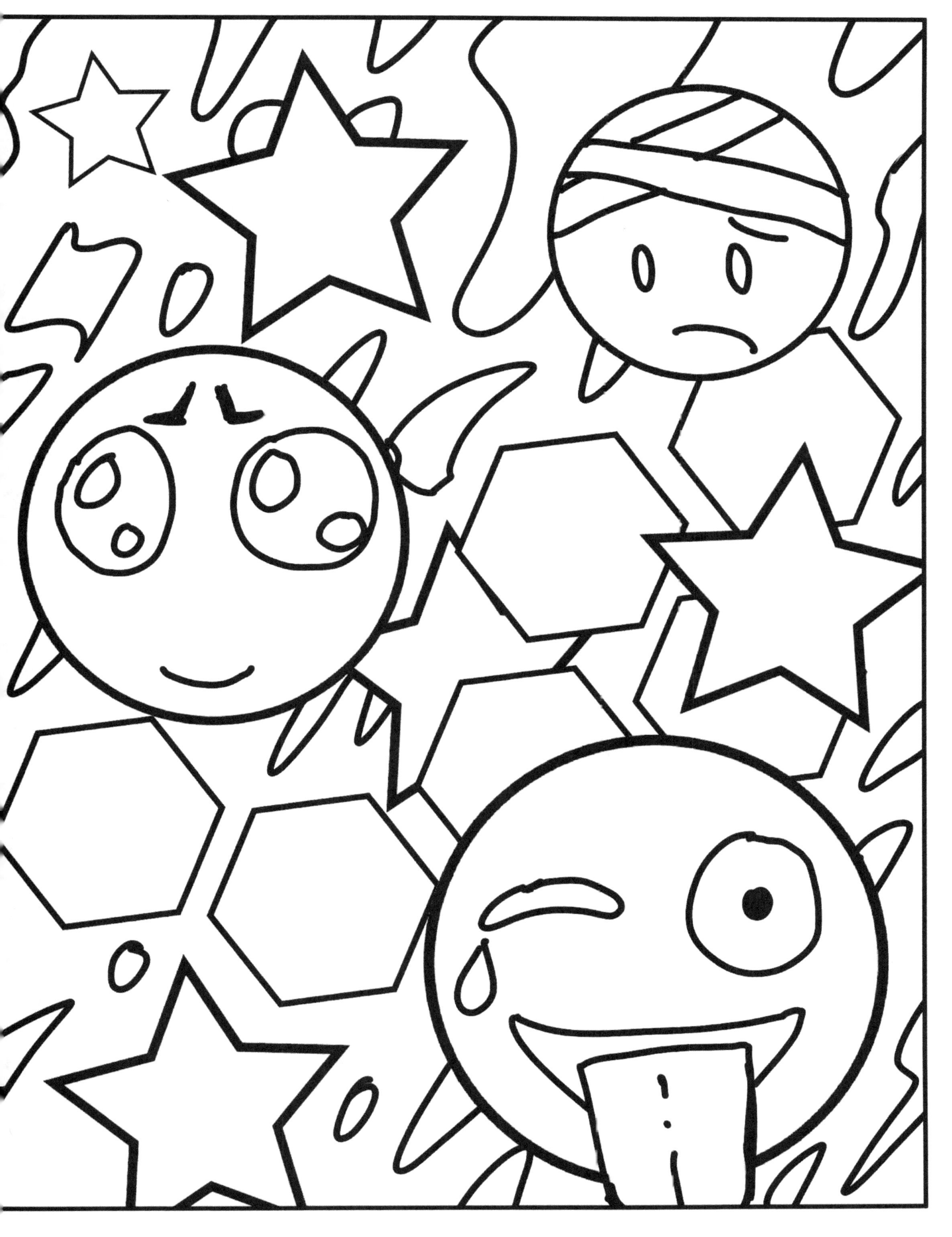

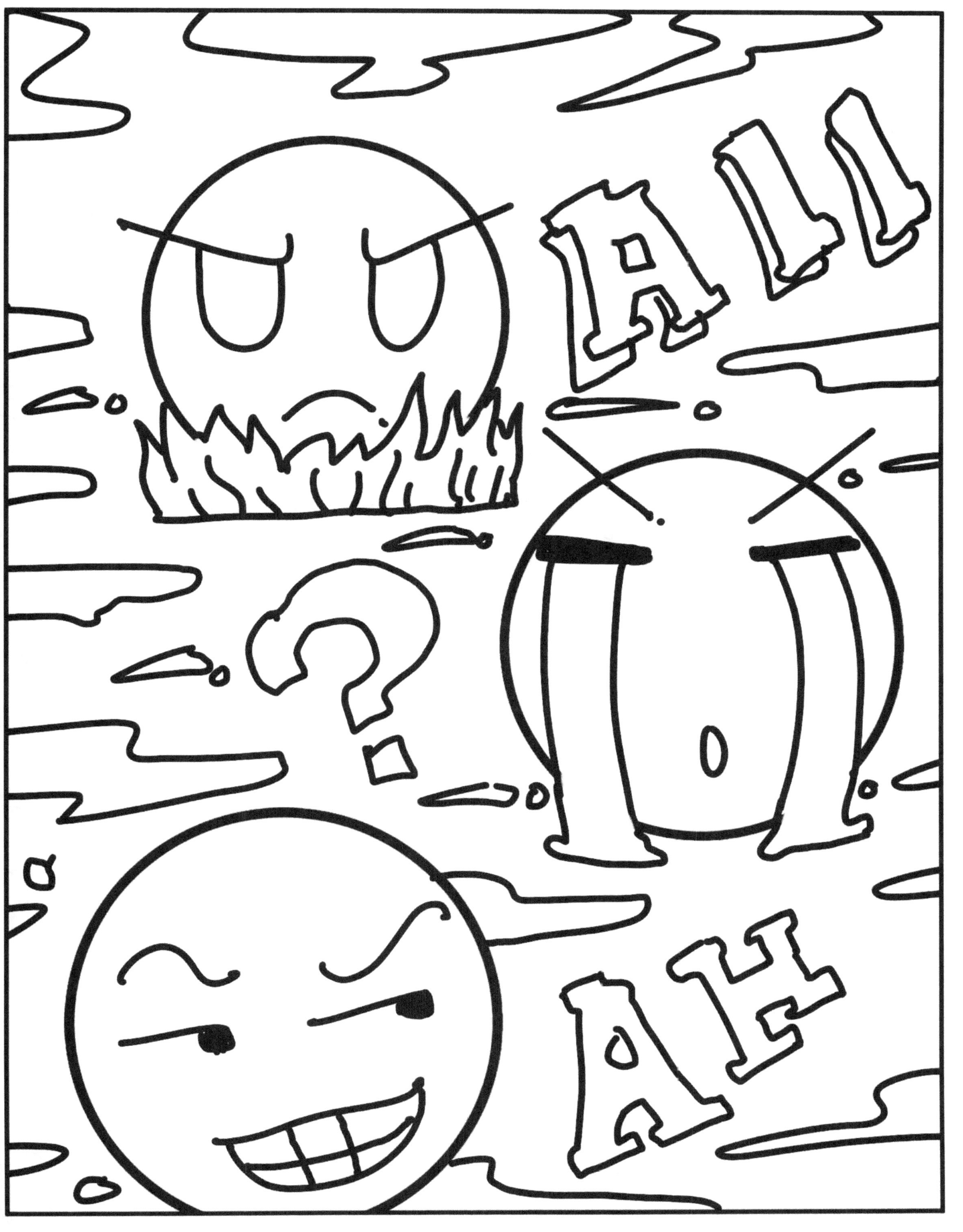

ALL
AH

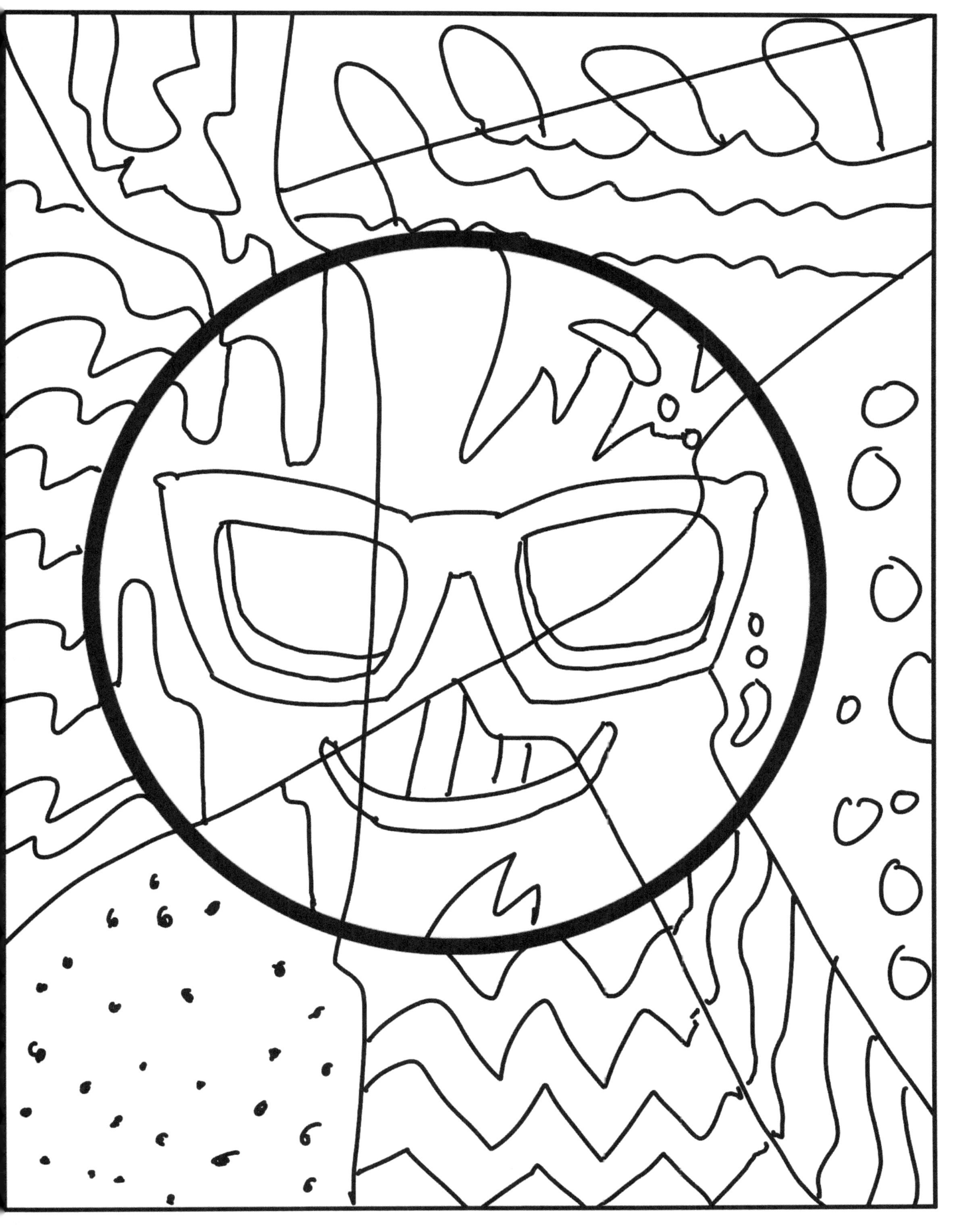

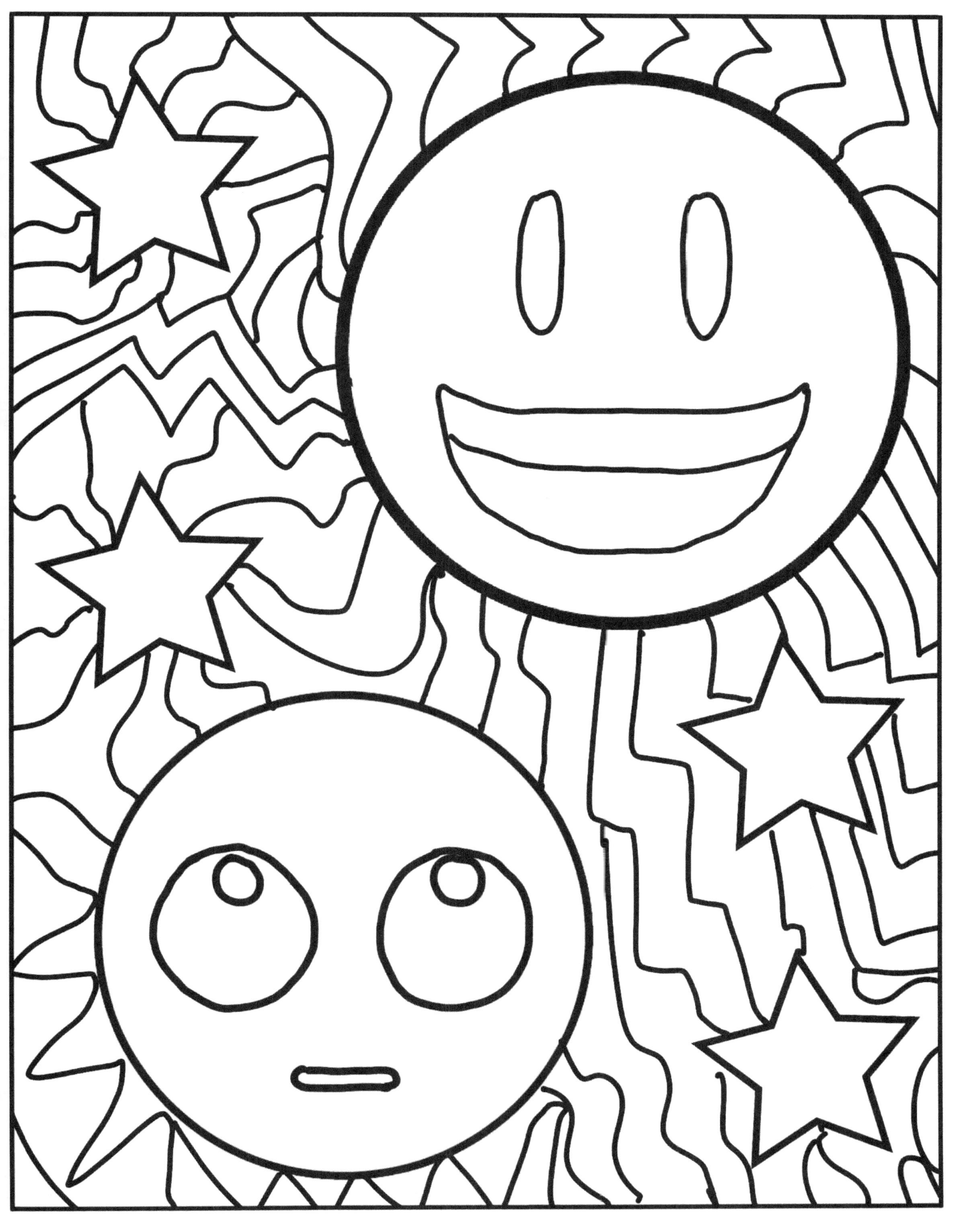

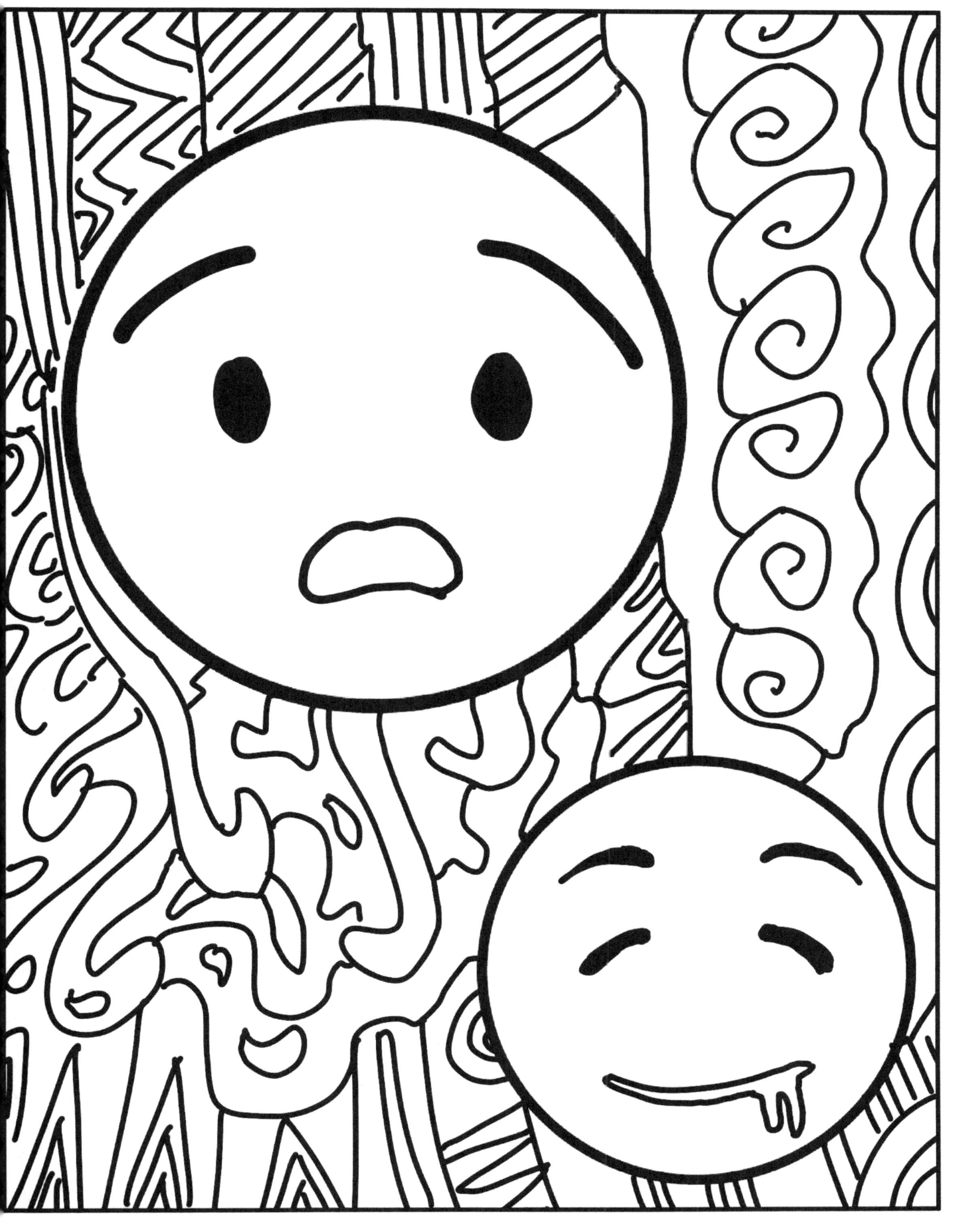

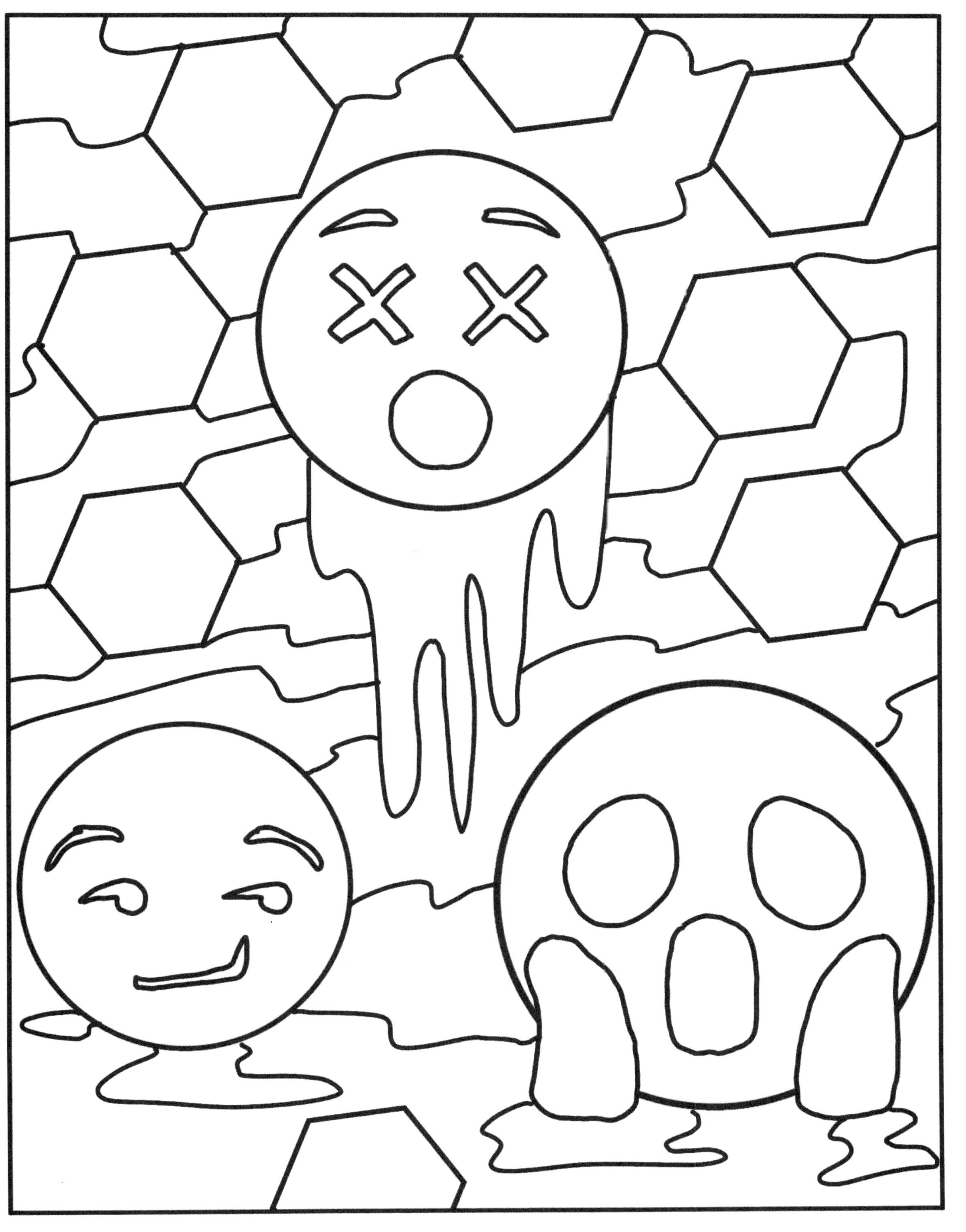

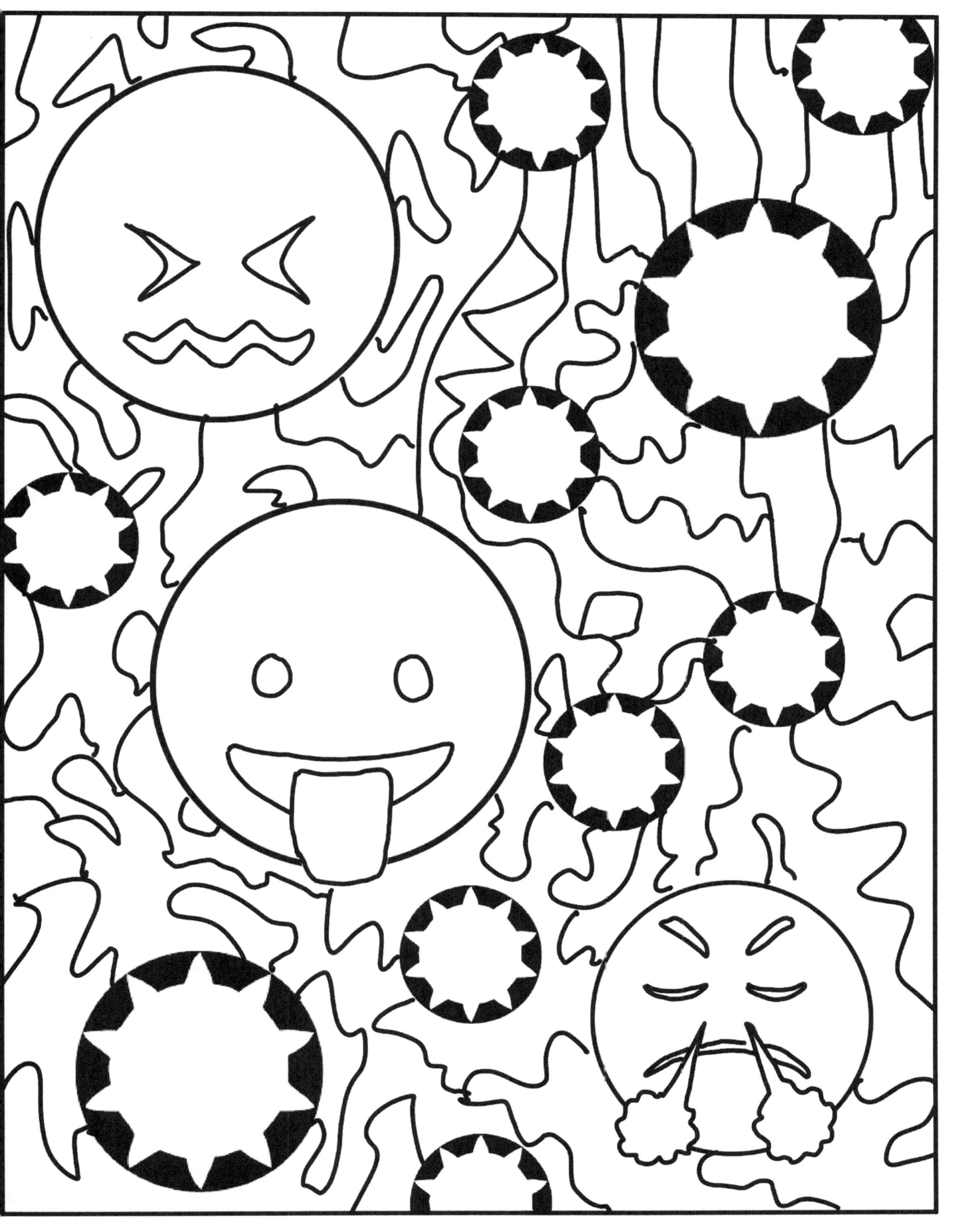

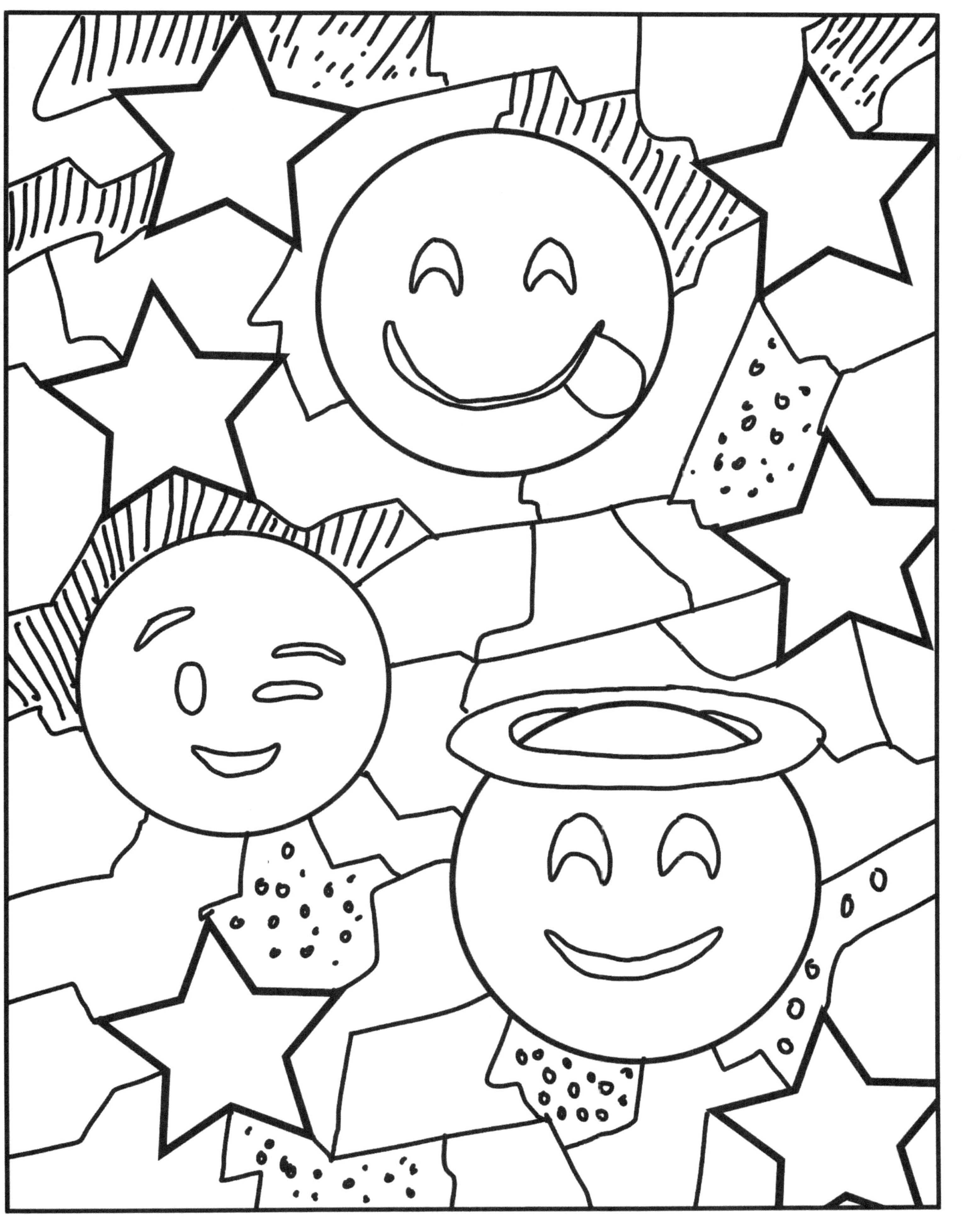

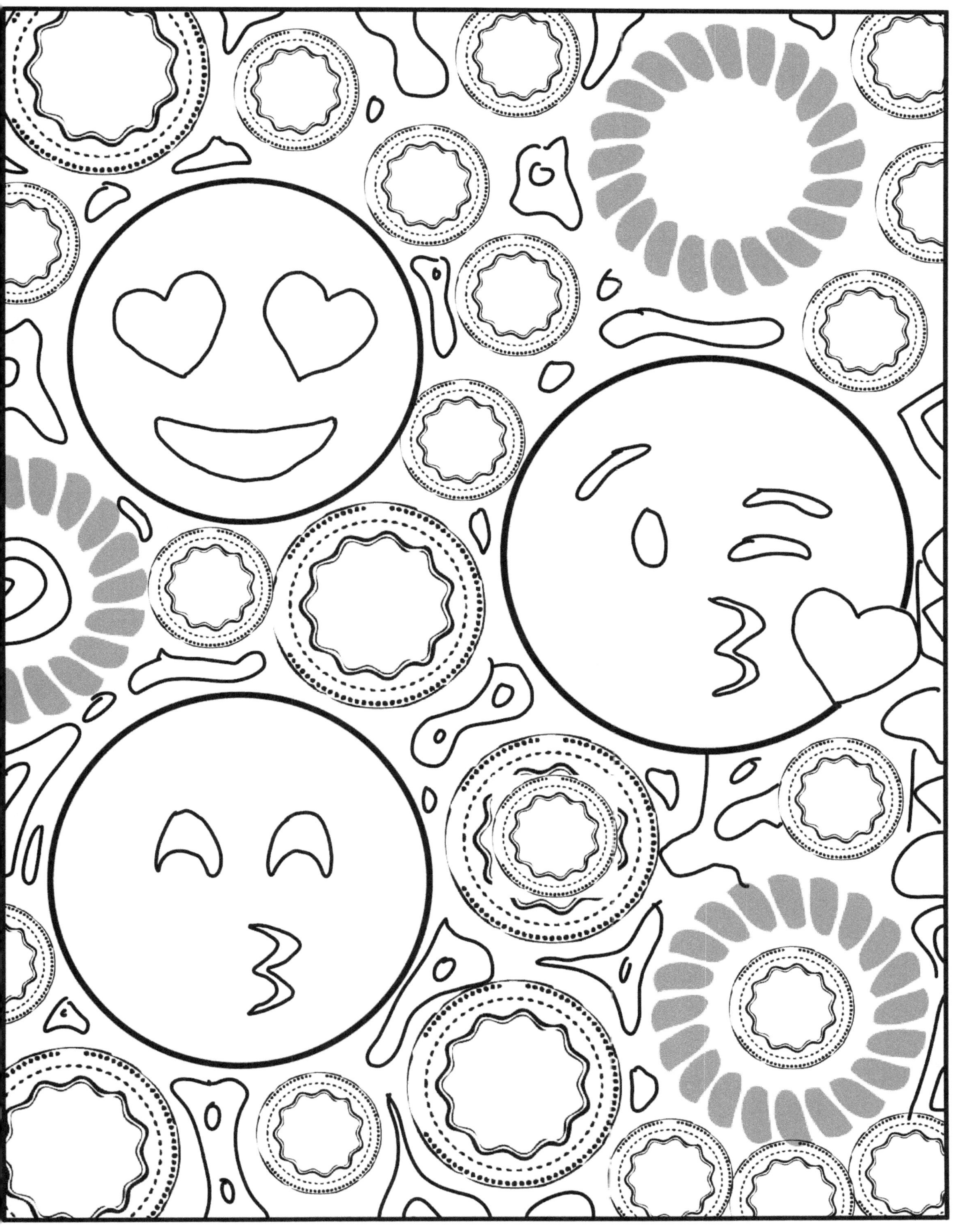

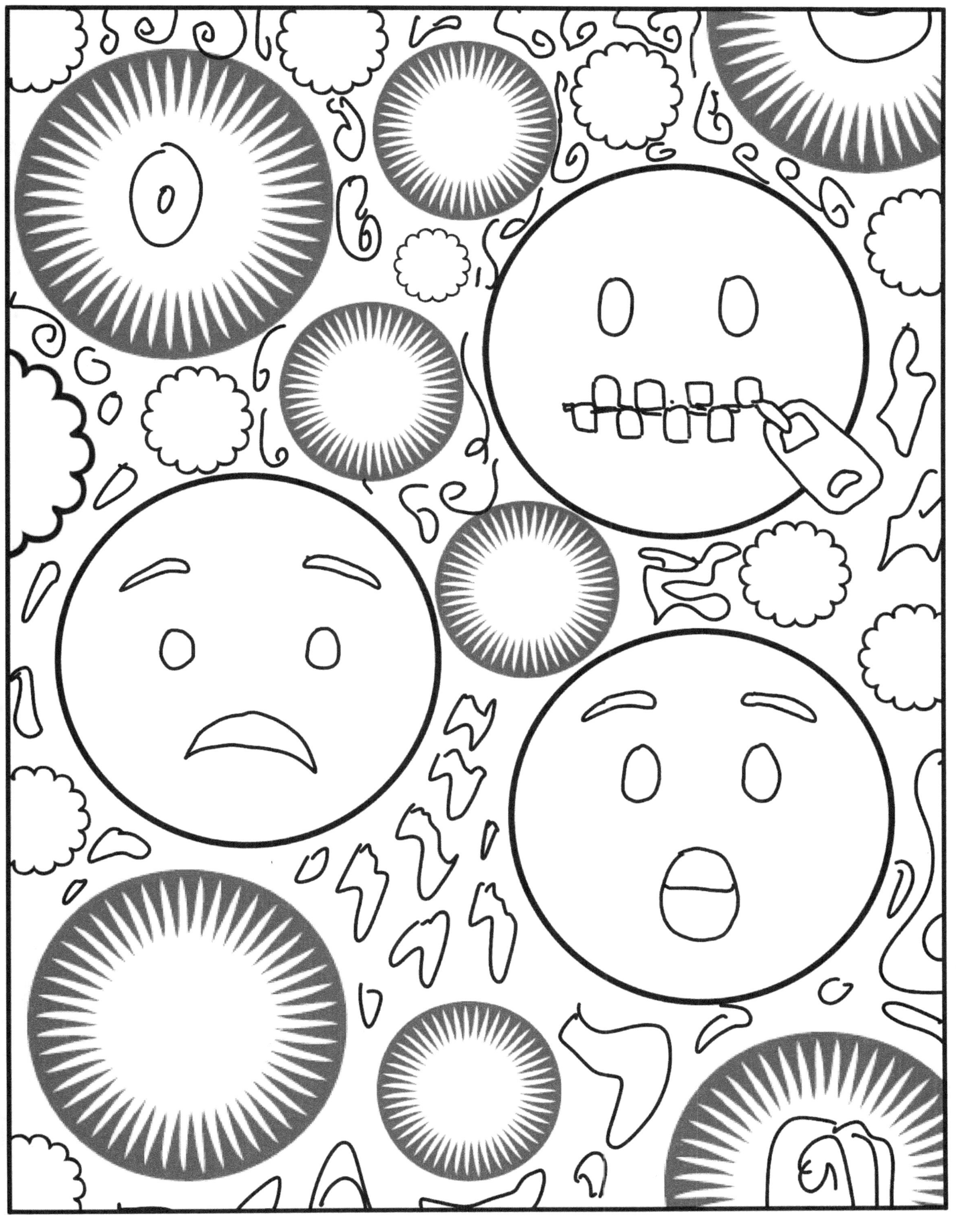

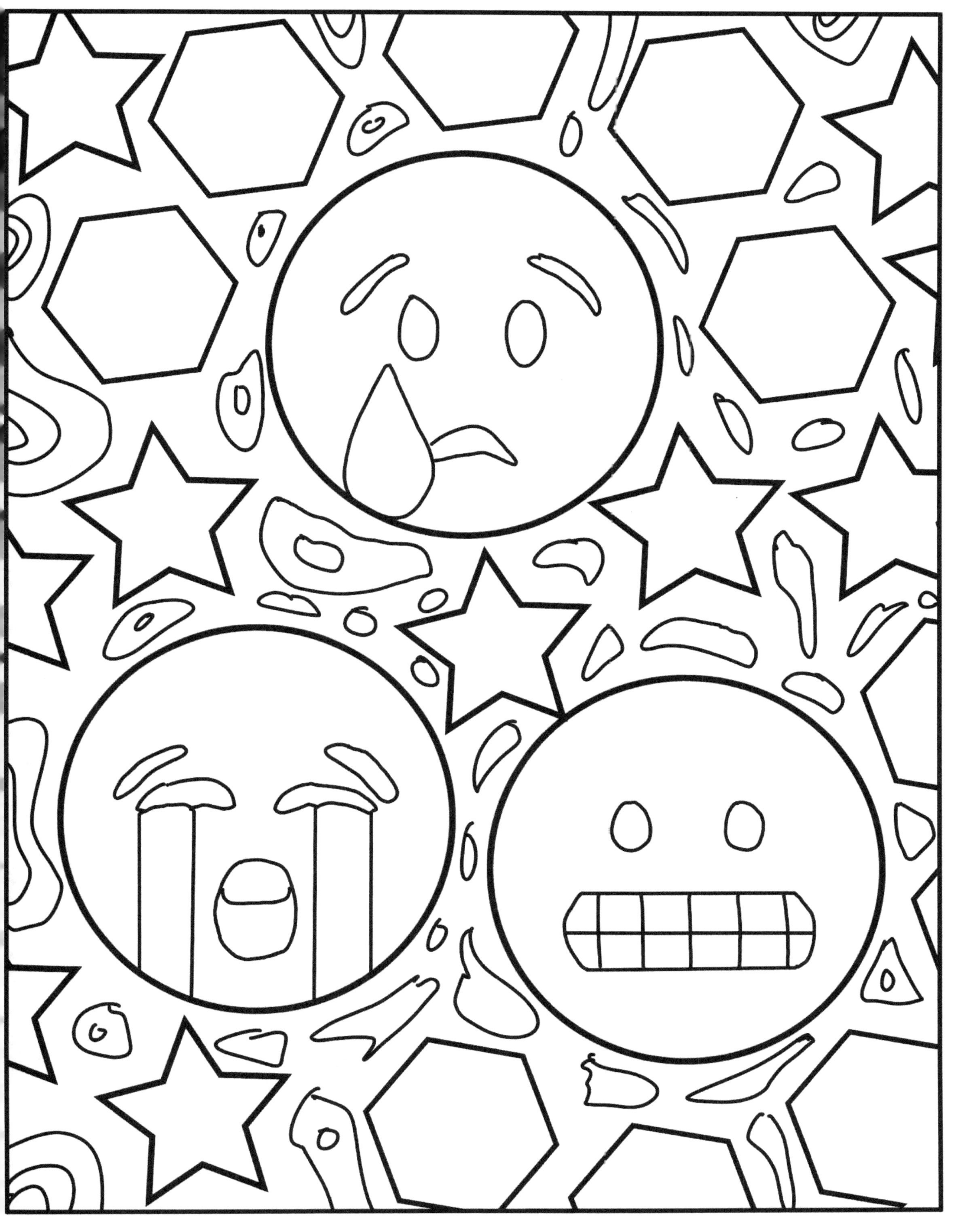

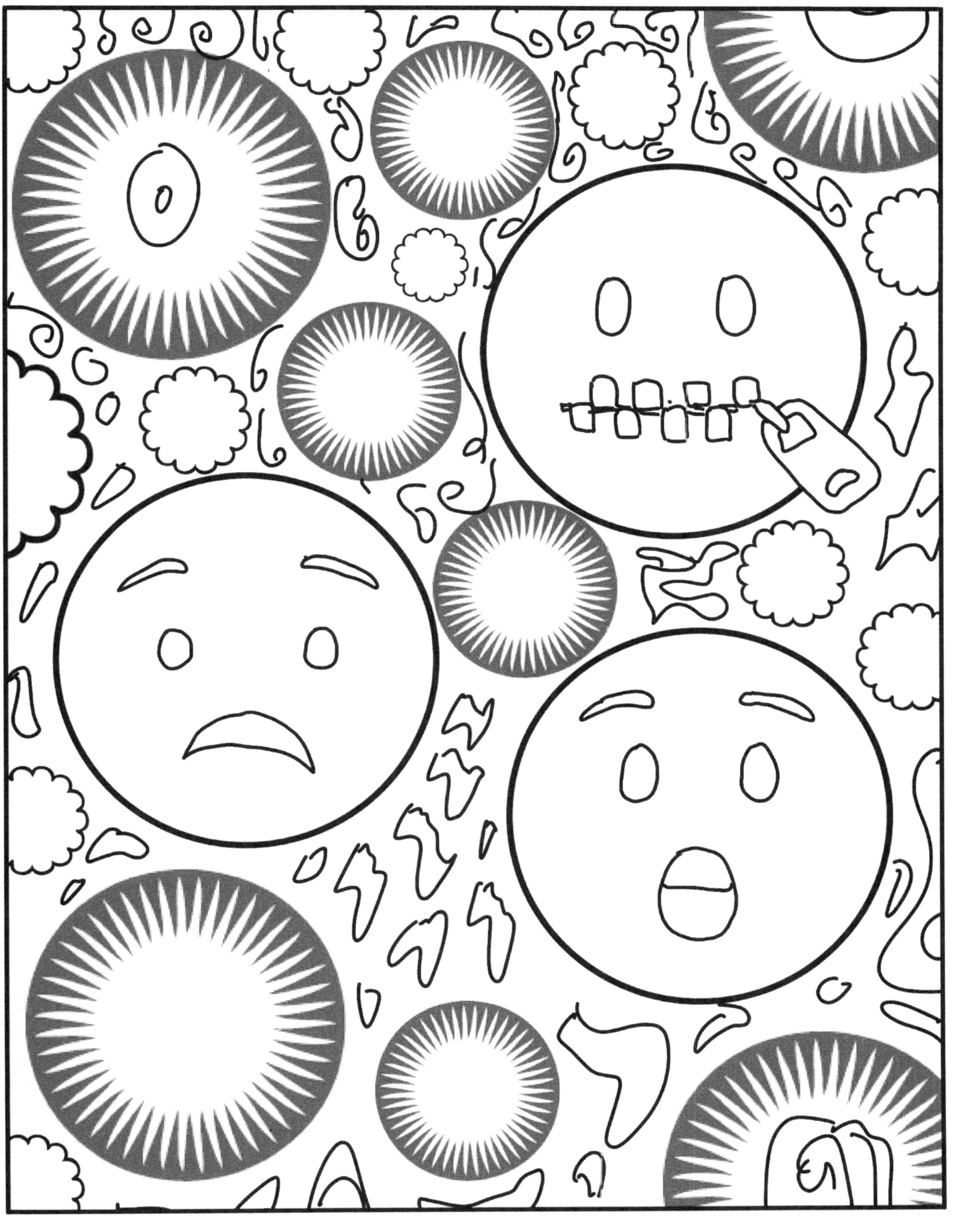

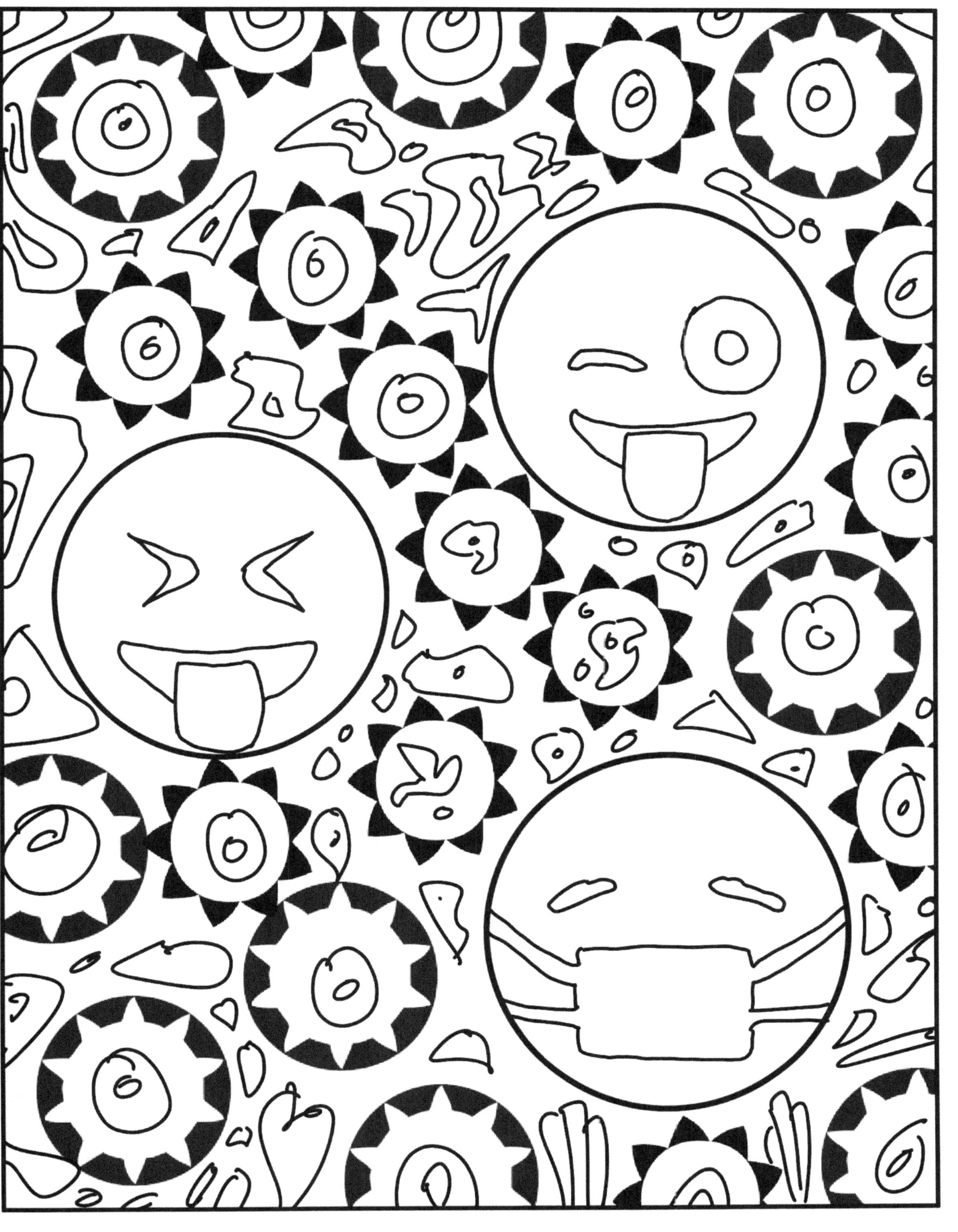

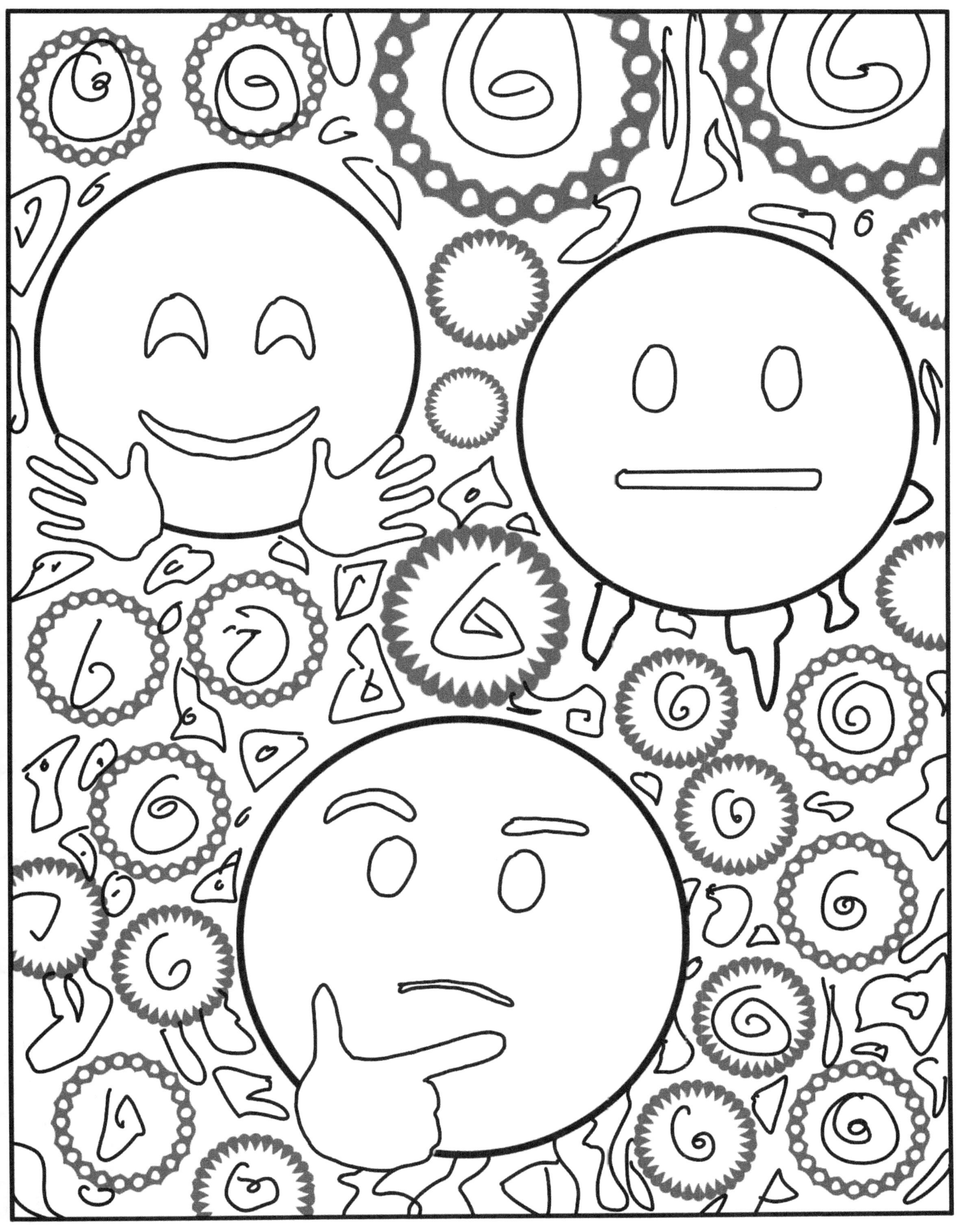

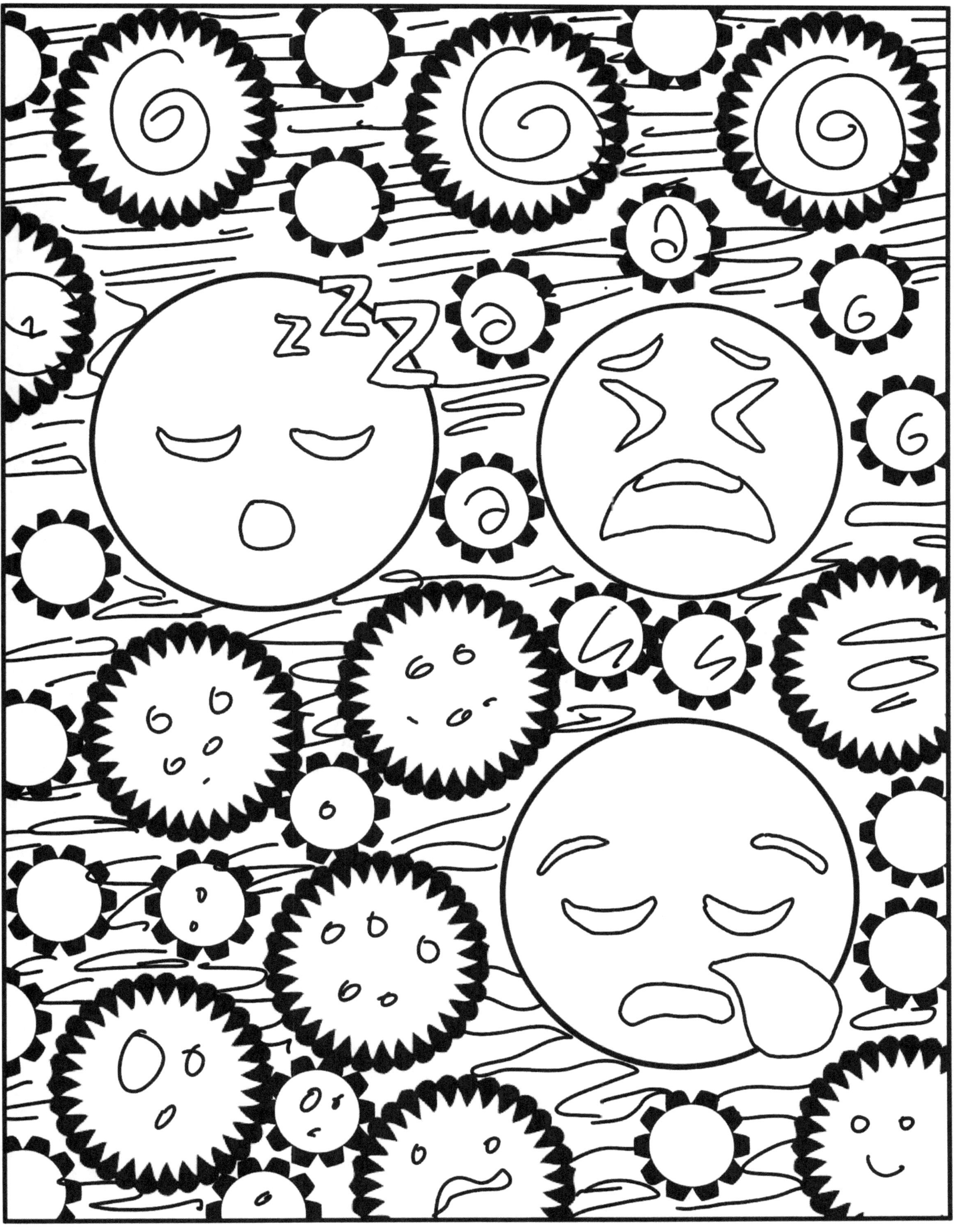

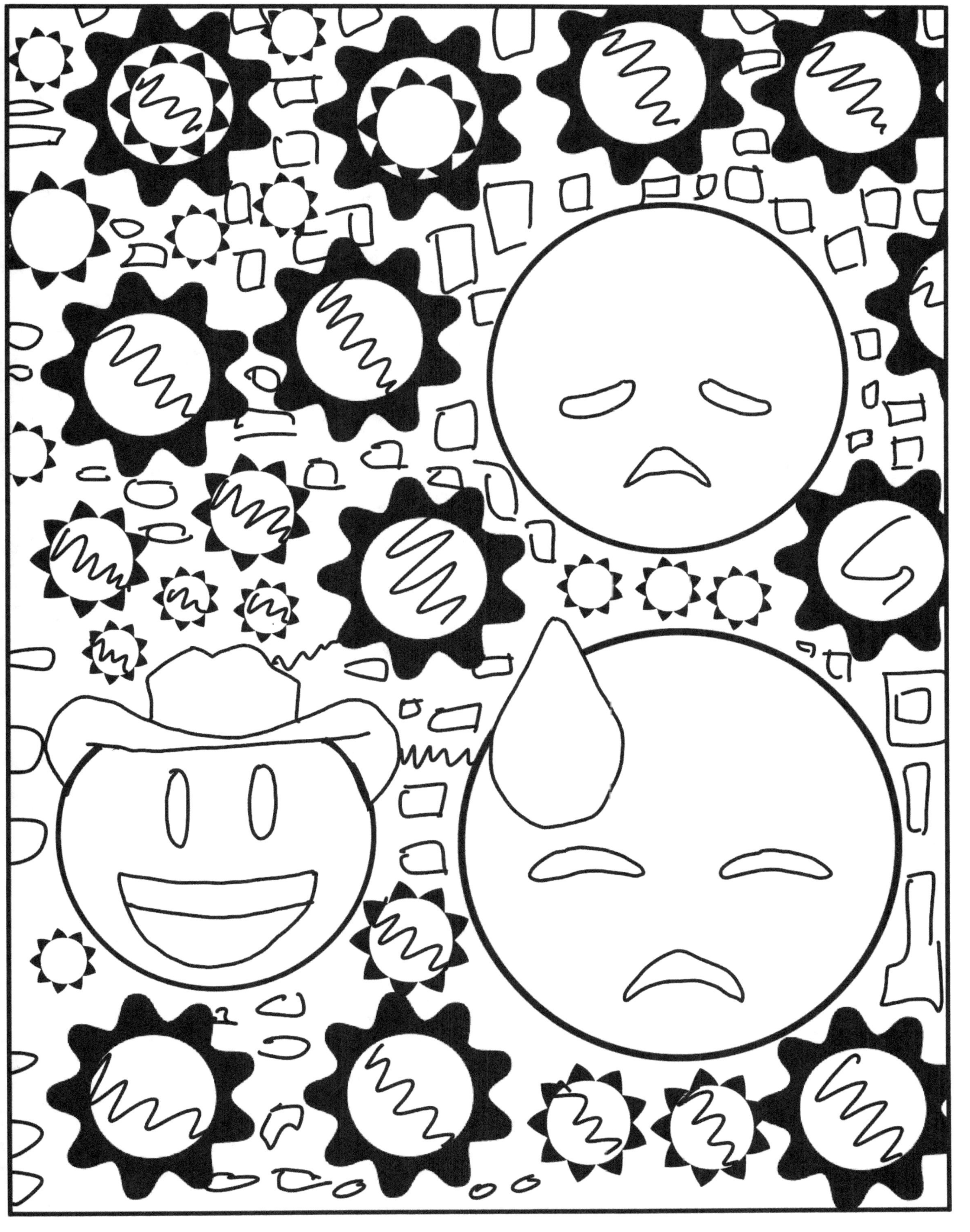

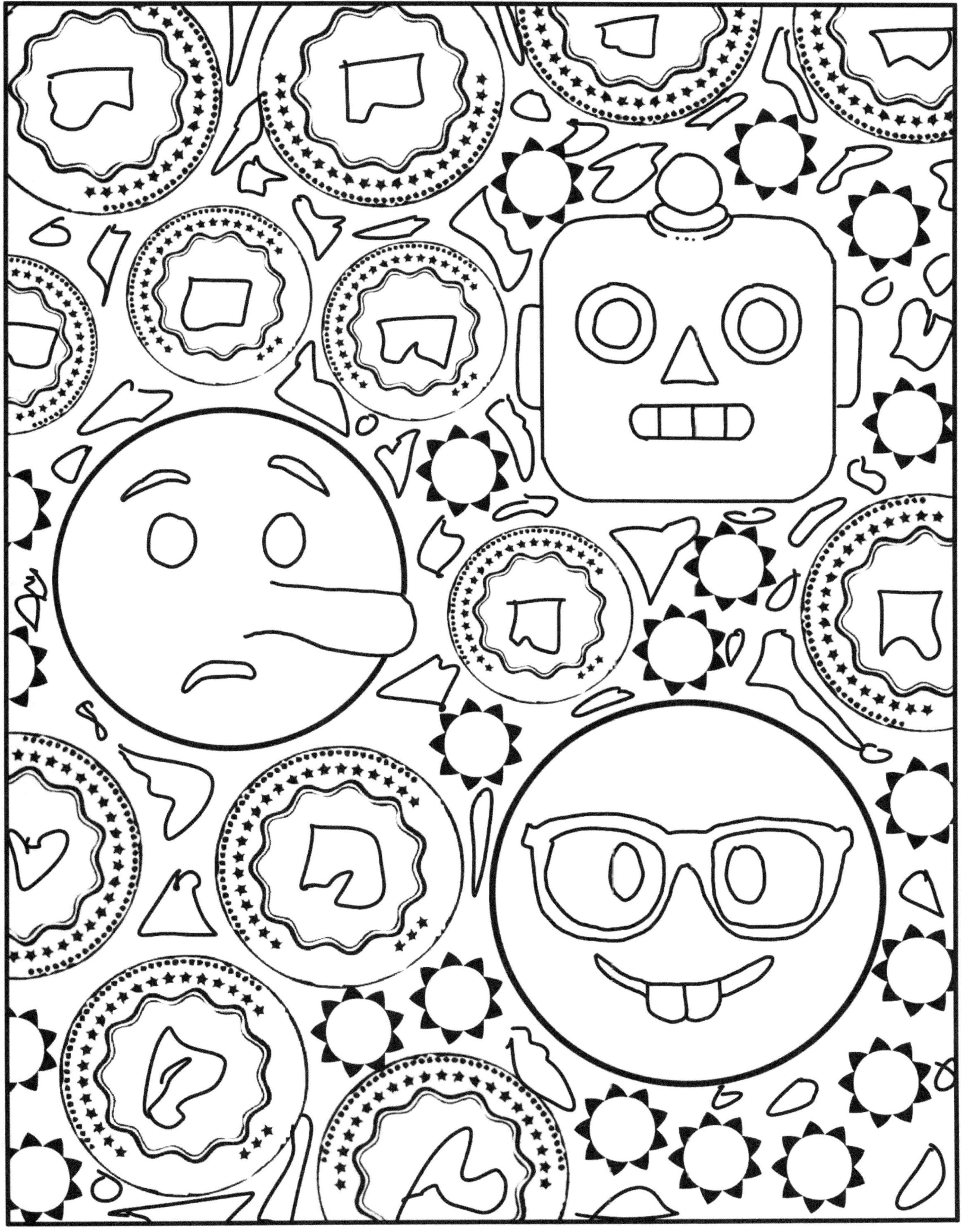

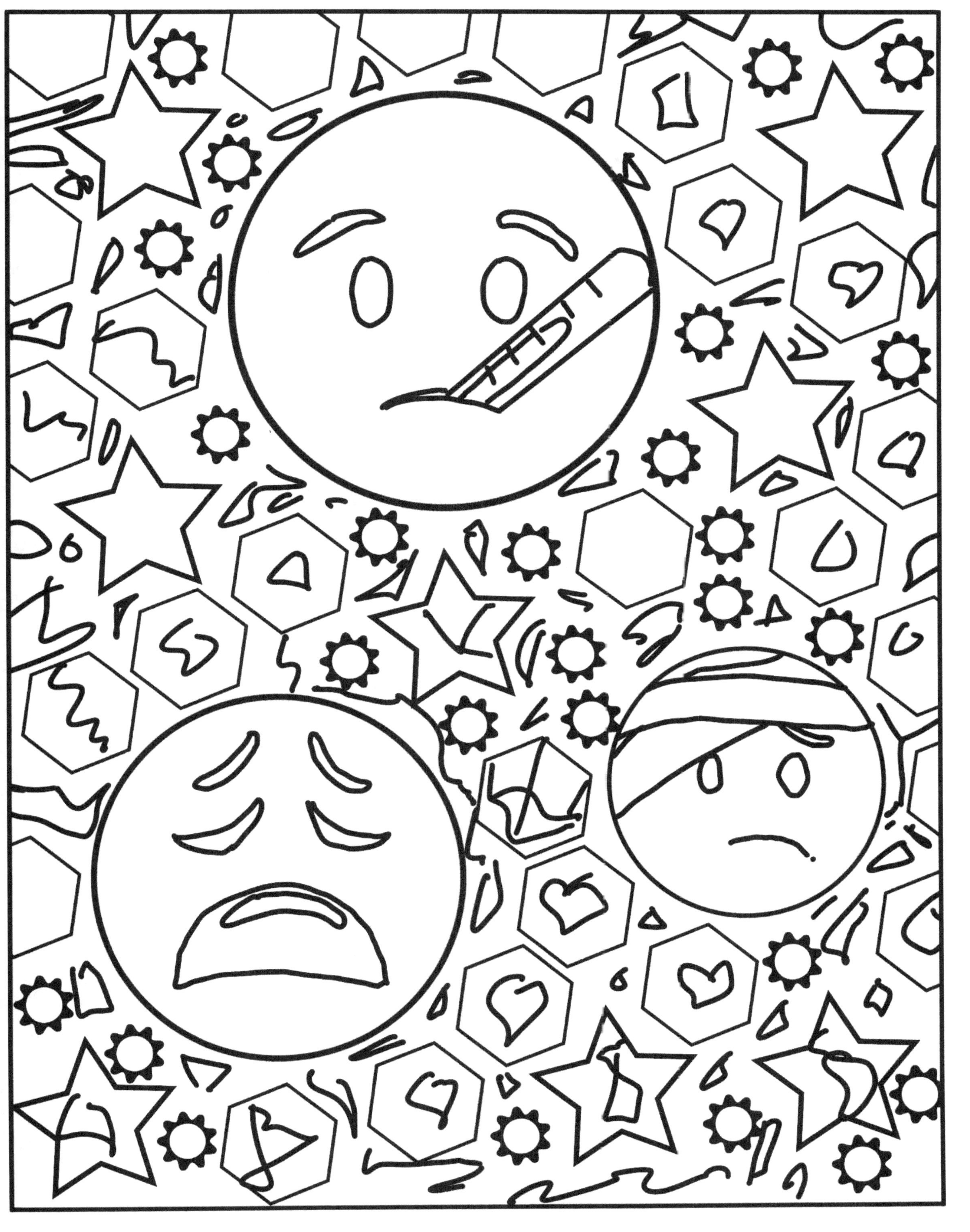

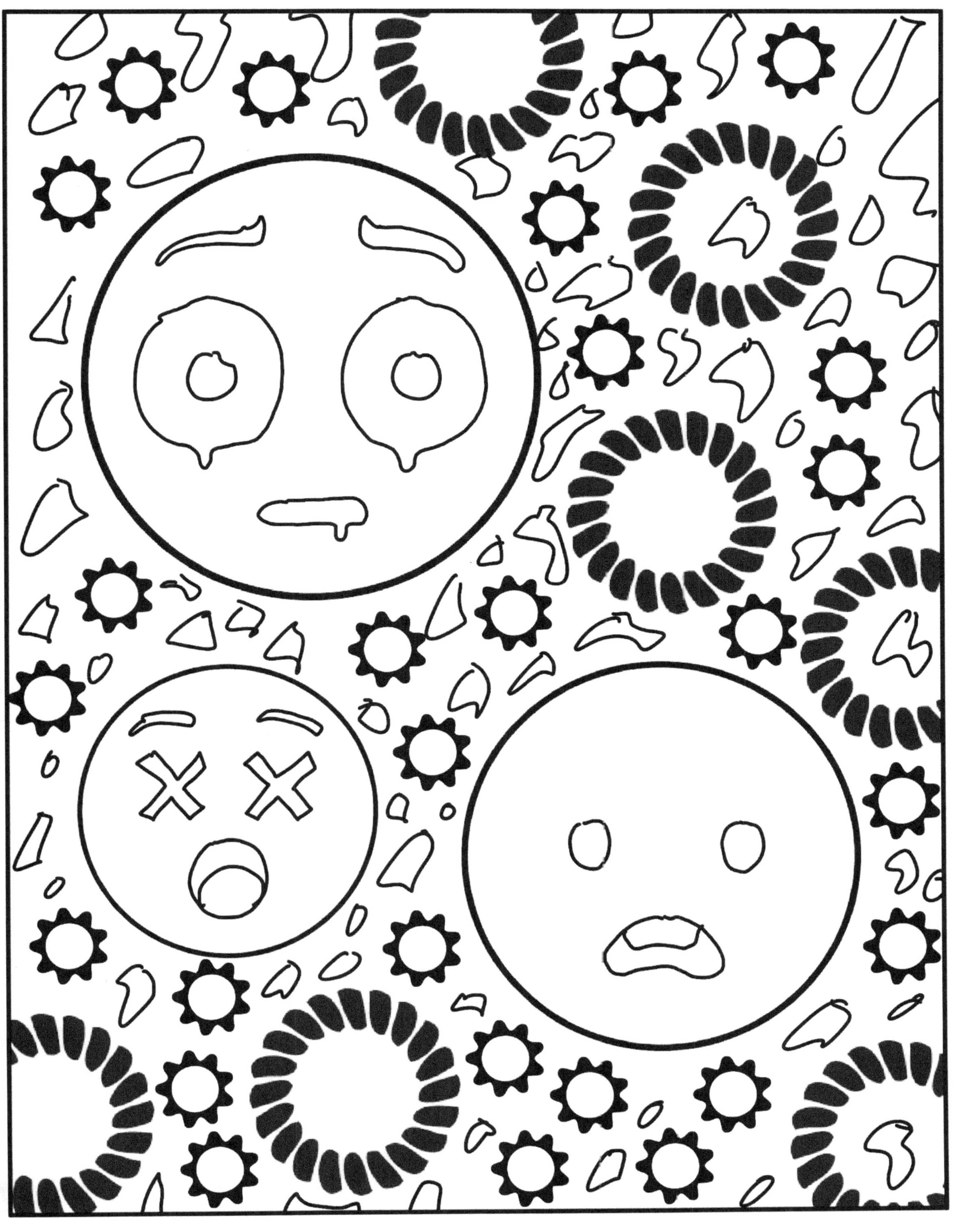

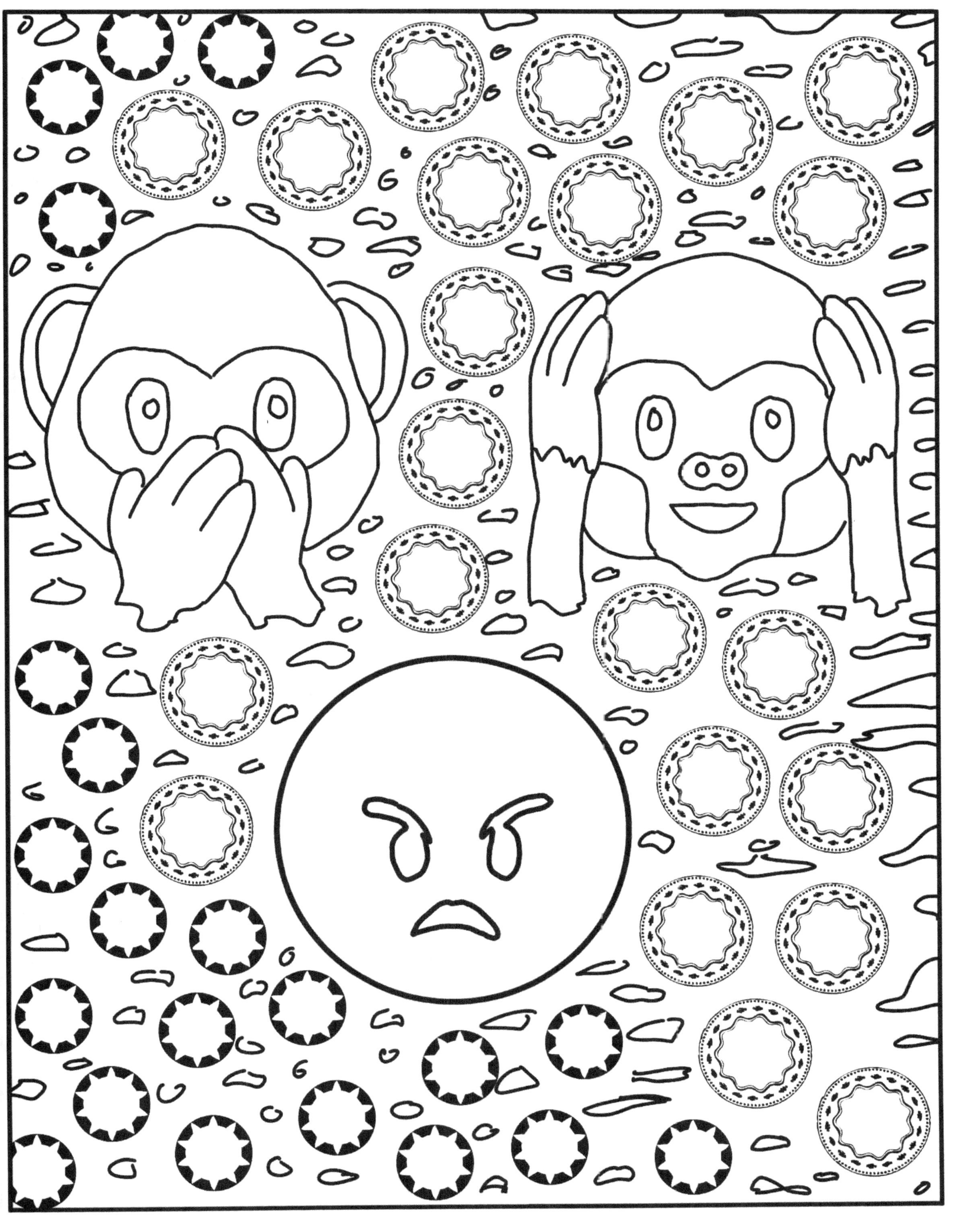

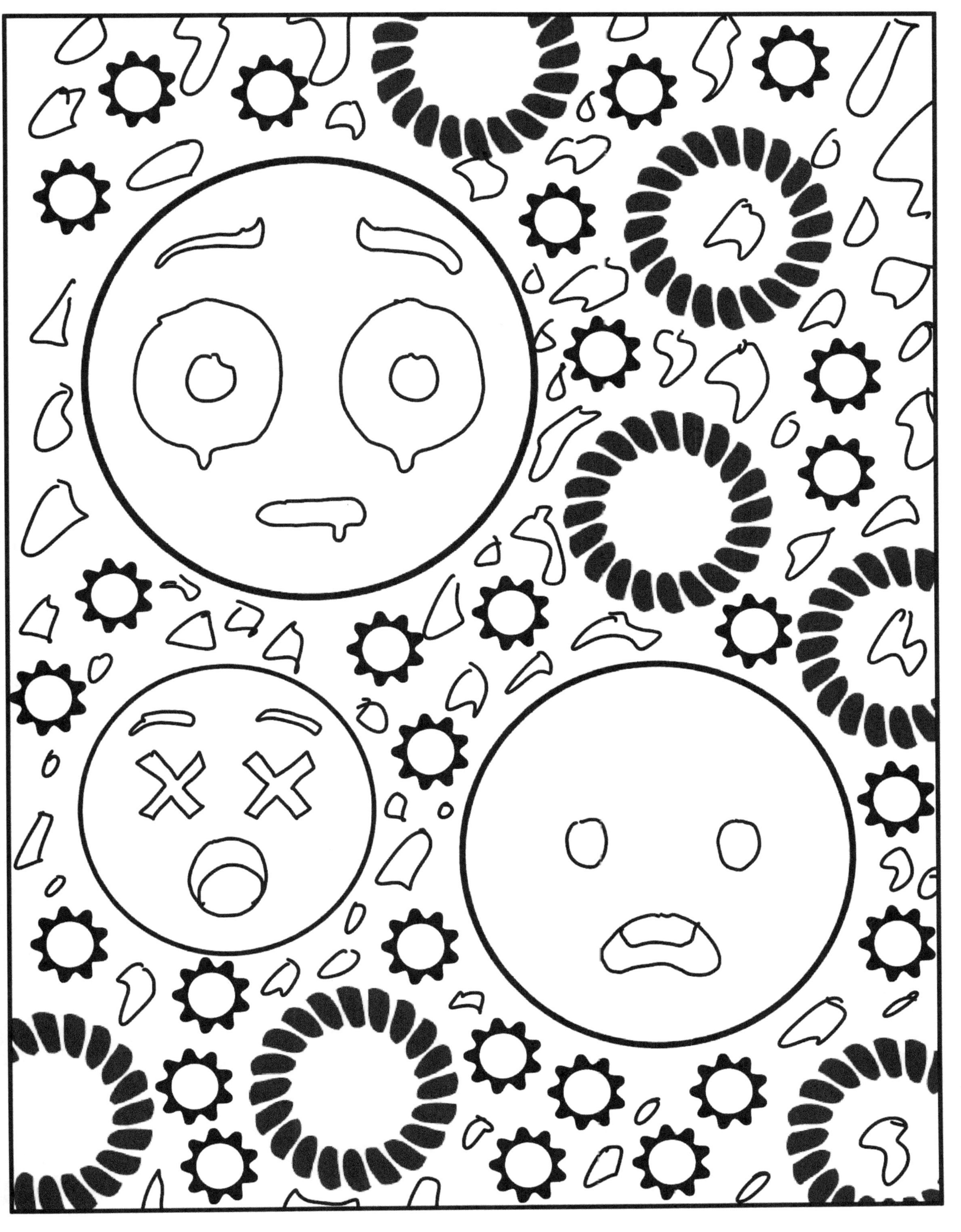

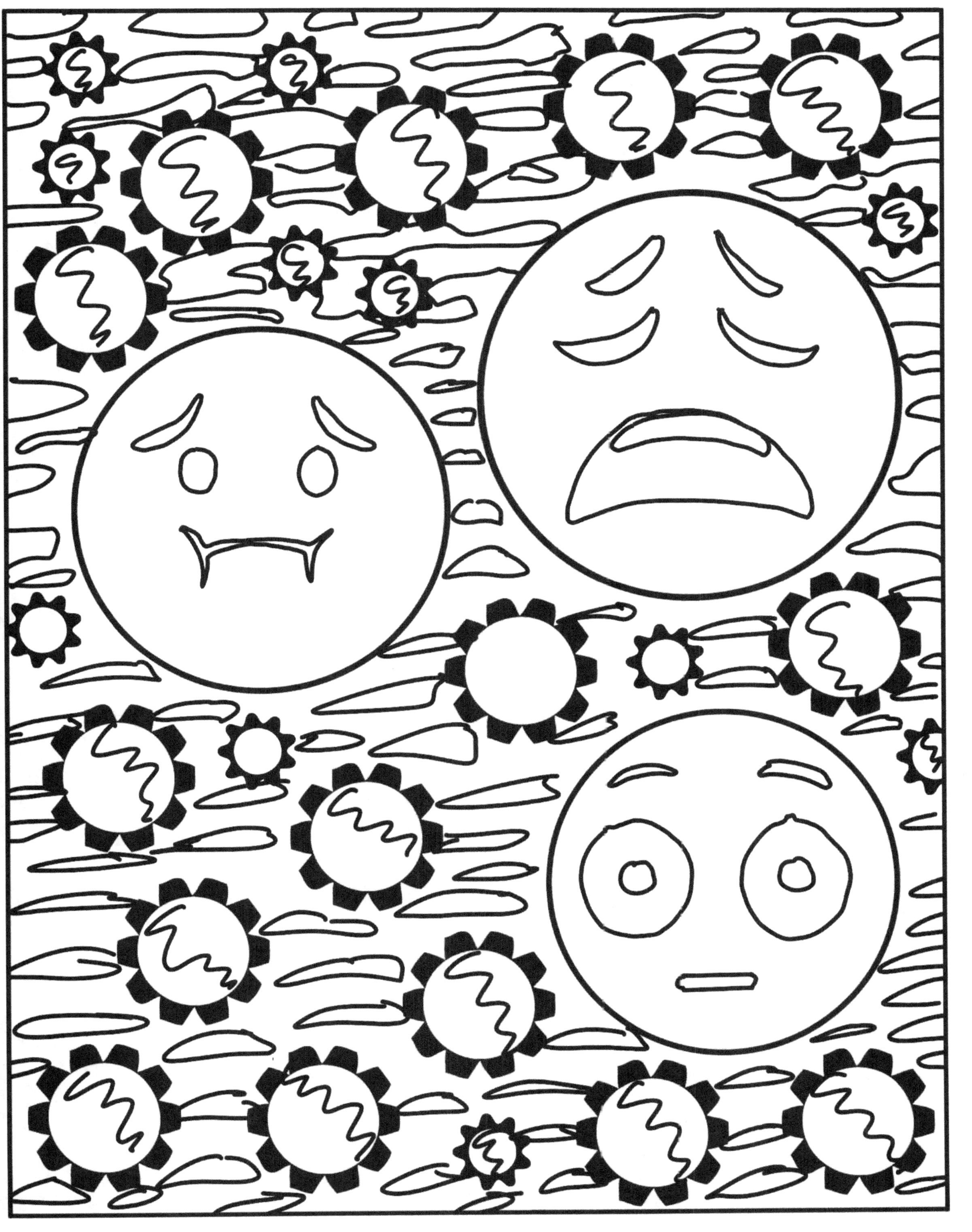

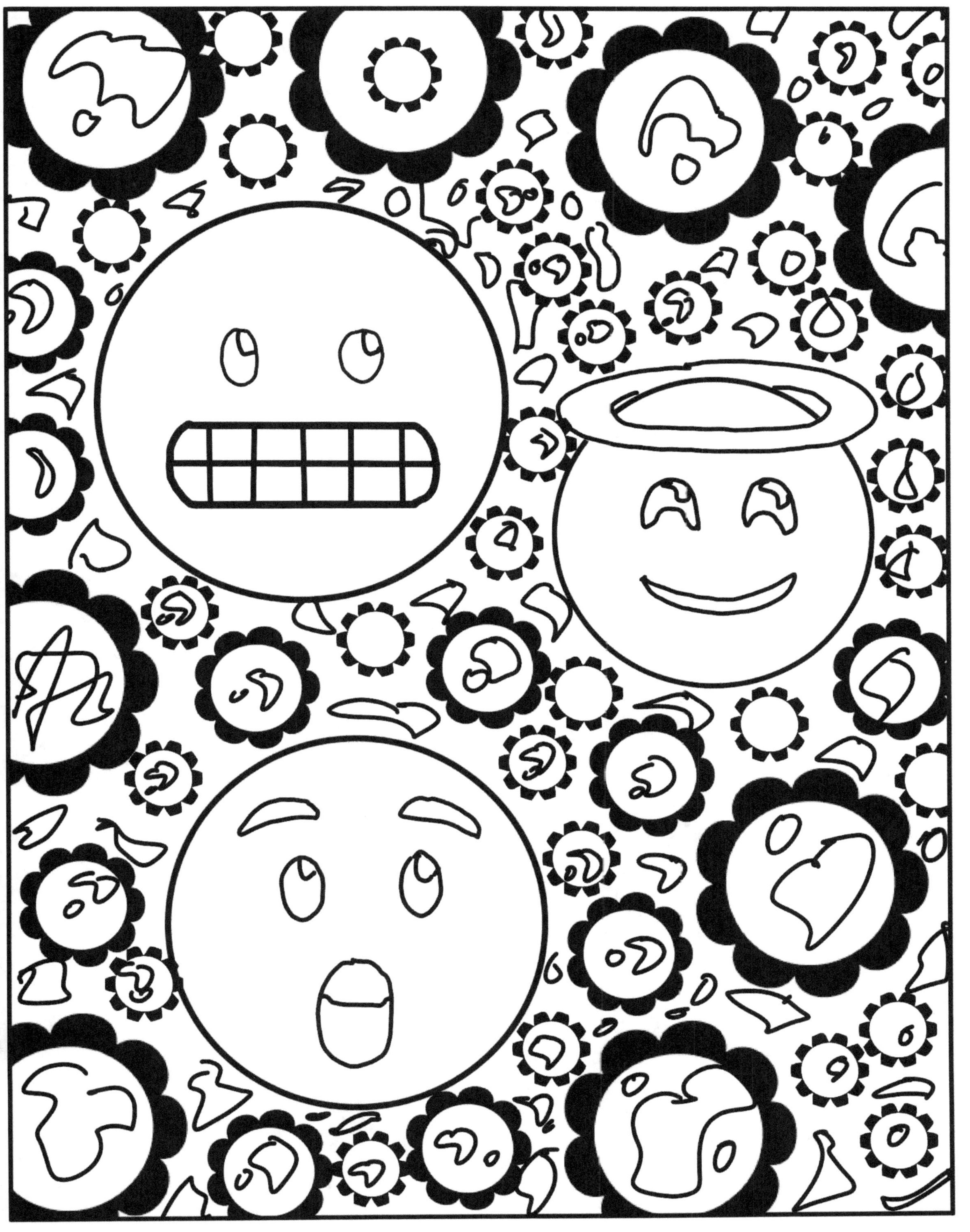

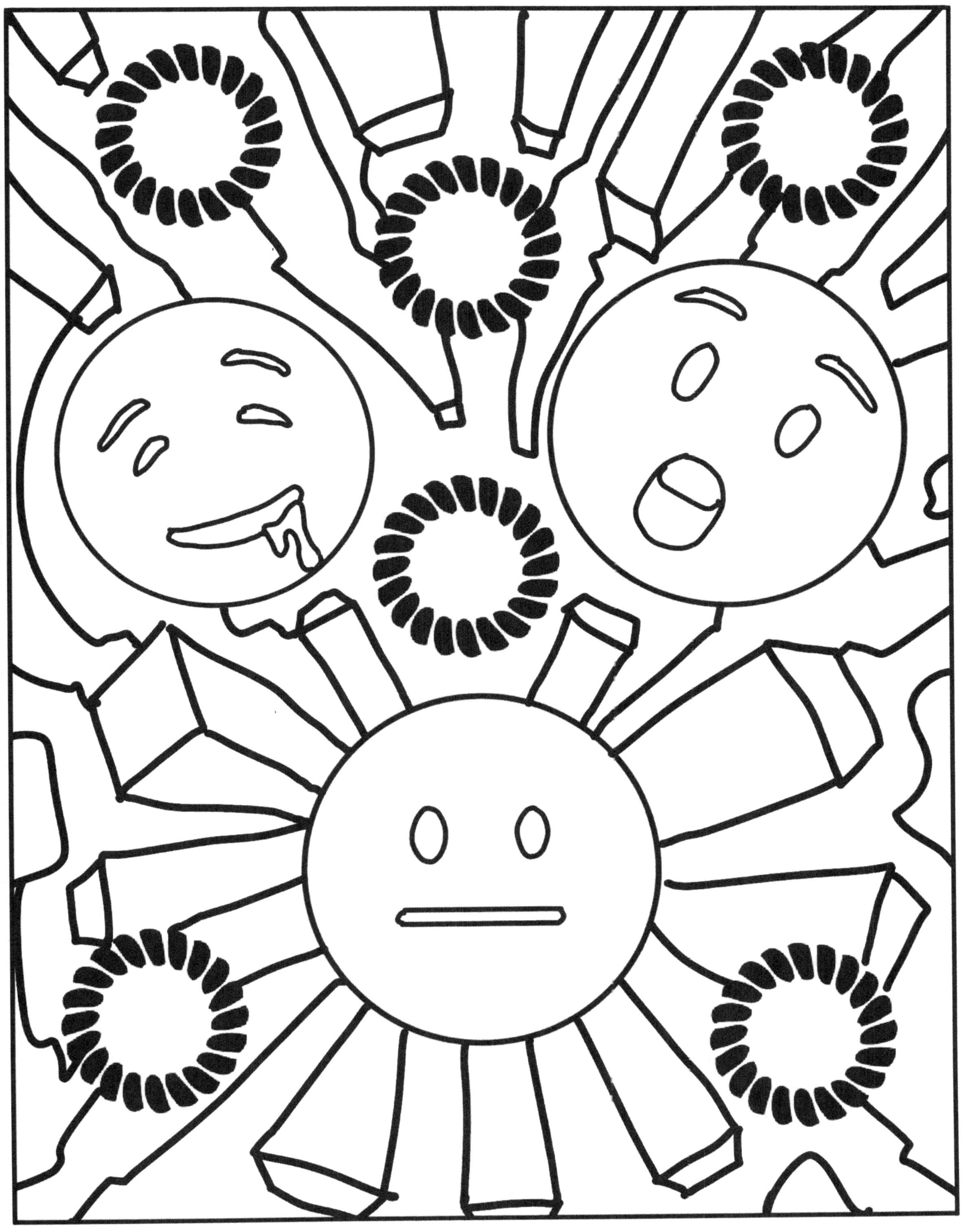

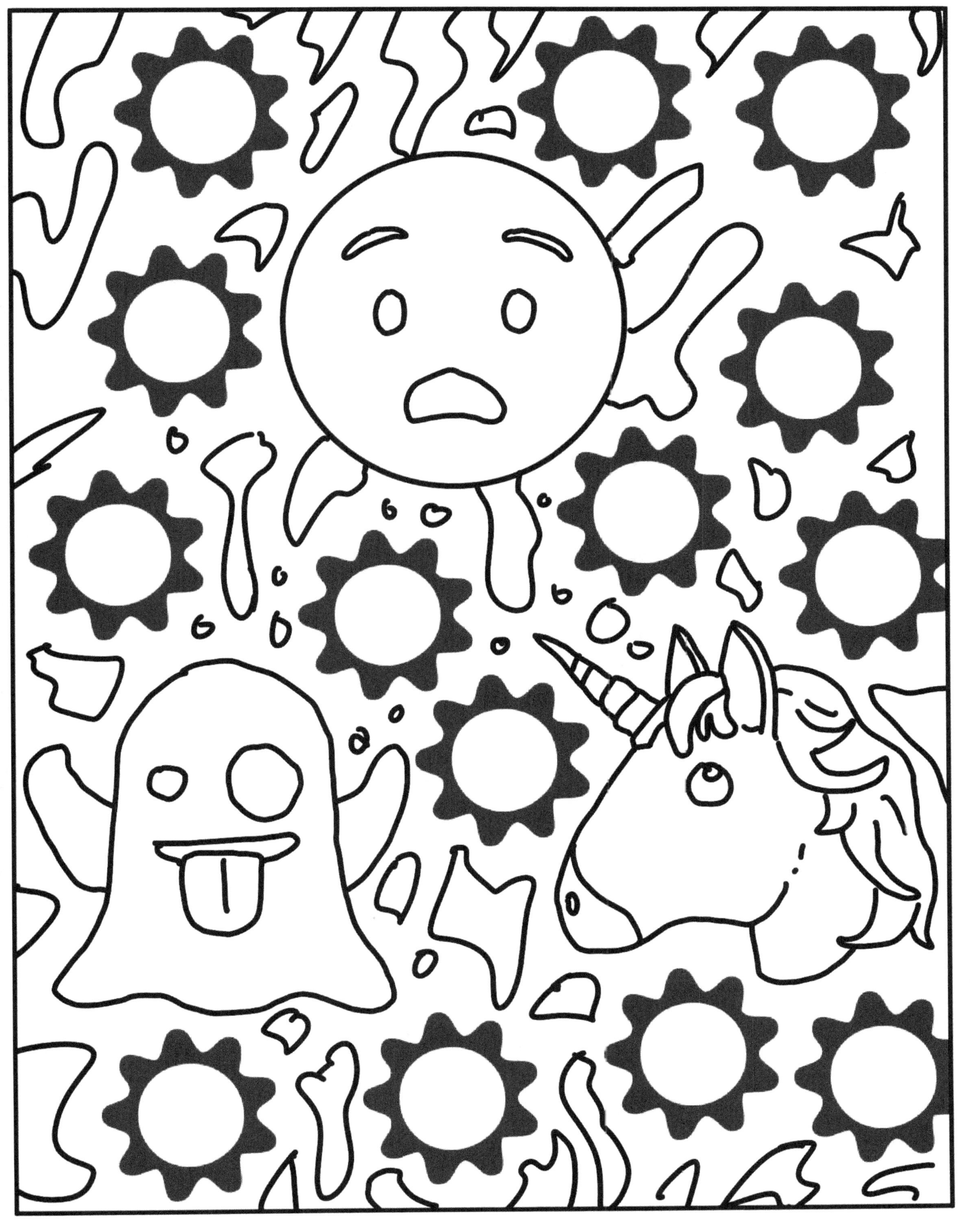

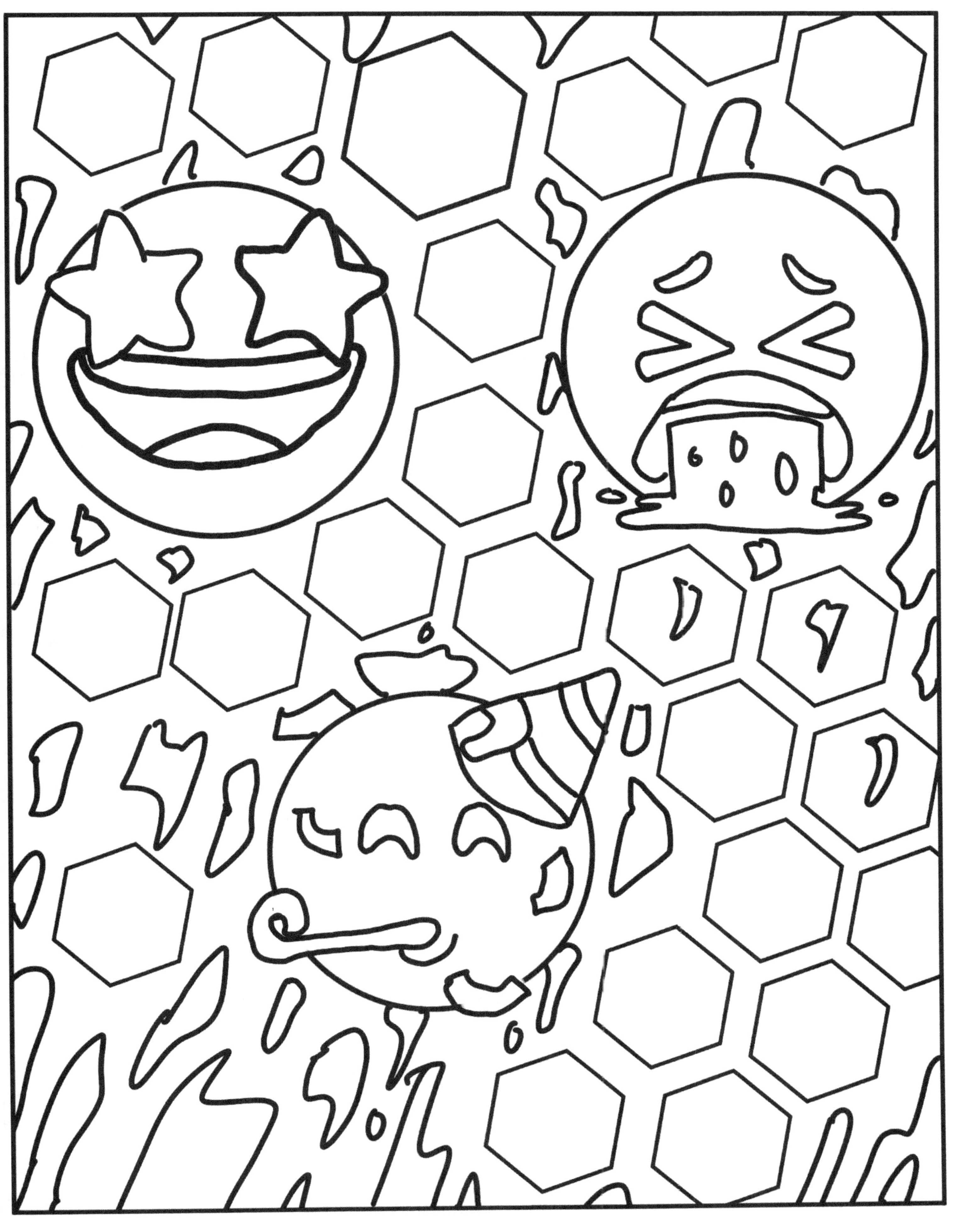

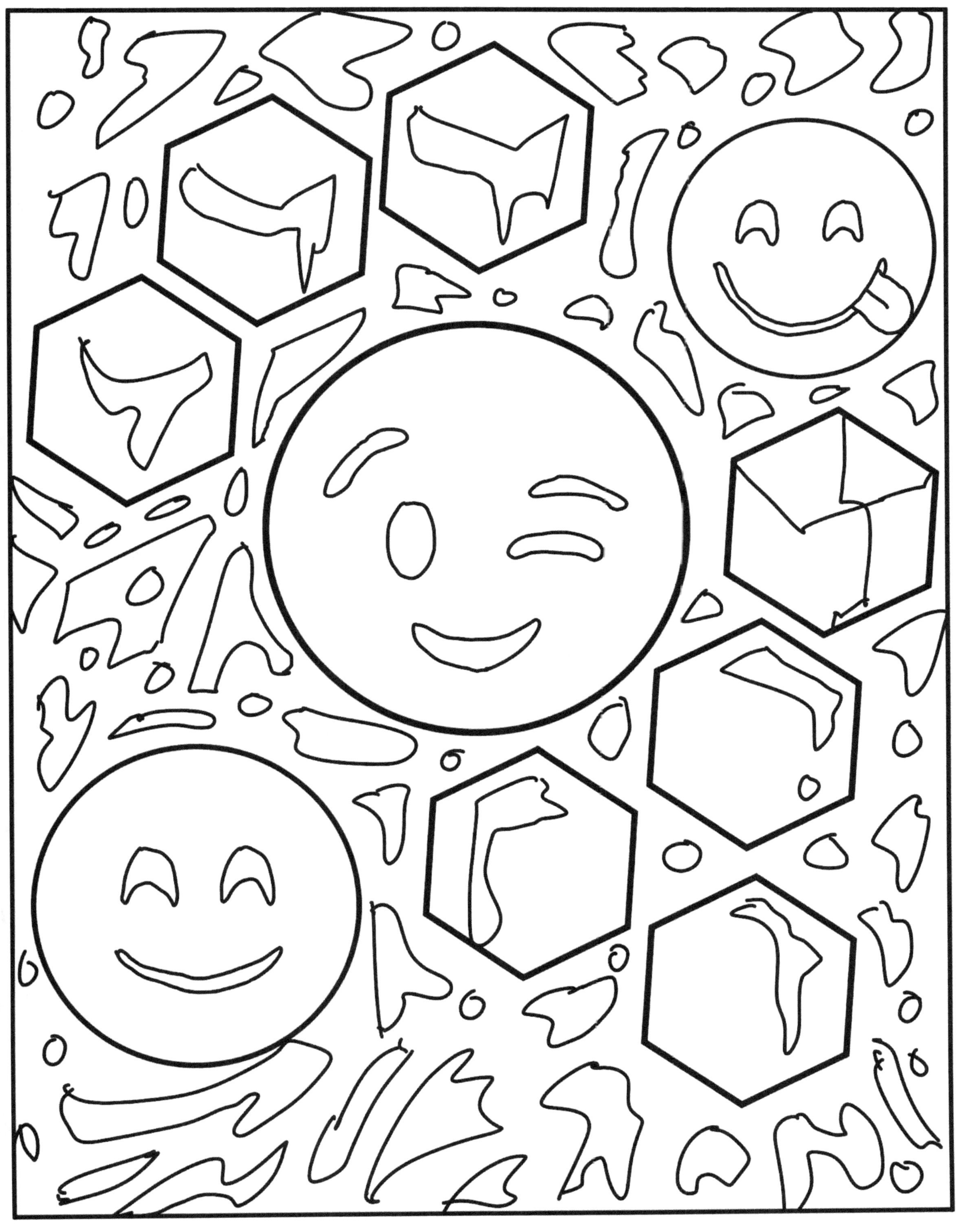